*Devotions, customs, and summertime activities*
*to celebrate the season of the Spirit*

# THE DAYS OF PENTECOST

## W. A. POOVEY

**AUGSBURG** Publishing House • Minneapolis

# Contents

# About This Book

Despite a renewed emphasis in the contemporary church on the work of the Holy Spirit, Pentecost and the days that follow it form a rather barren stretch of the church year for many people. This book seeks to provide material that will give the reader a greater appreciation for the days of Pentecost.

There are three sections to the book. Part I concentrates on the events of Pentecost and then takes a quick look at the rest of the non-festival part of the church year.

Part II talks about the Christian in summer. It contains suggestions of how the believer can be led into deeper faith even when the church schedule and one's personal feelings may be more directed toward vacations and relaxation.

Part III contains thirty brief devotions based on passages that speak about the Holy Spirit. The devotions are not intended to provide a systematic discussion of church doctrine. Rather each seeks to make plain what the Bible has to say about this third member of the Triune God.

May the Spirit of God guide you to find help and inspiration during these days of Pentecost.

PART I | **The Story of Pentecost**

# Last of the Big Three

We say "Merry Christmas" when that festival arrives. We wish people a "Happy Easter." But no one says, "Peppy Pentecost." No one asks, "Are you ready for Pentecost?" The secular world, which has almost taken over Christmas and is exploiting Easter with clothing and candy, has left Pentecost strictly alone. This is a blessing except that it indicates the low ranking of the last of the big three Christian festivals. Pentecost, which occurs fifty days after Easter marks Christ's gift of the Holy Spirit to his followers. It is the official birthday of the Christian church. Pentecost marks the transition from the festival to the non-festival half of the church year. Yet when a survey was made of a congregation 78% of the members couldn't think of a single thing to say about Pentecost.

Perhaps the reason for this neglect is partly the festival itself. Christmas, with its story of a child born in a stable and with its cast of angels and shepherds and wise men seems ready-made for a sentimental holiday. Easter not only brings us the astonishing news—He is Risen—but is also accompanied by the arrival of spring, a longed-for event, especially in cold climates. Even those who do not know the risen Lord look forward to the coming of Easter.

But Pentecost—the story is spectacular, but it is difficult to understand. The Holy Spirit is mysterious, hard to define and often a subject of controversy among Christians. We can understand the bewilderment of the Japanese gentleman, as narrated by Dorothy Sayers in *The Mind of the Maker* who says, "Honourable Father, very good; Honourable Son, very good; but Honourable Bird, I do not understand at all."

To add that Pentecost is the birthday of the church doesn't cause us to sing "Happy Birthday" to anyone either, for we tend to identify the church with our own congregation or denomination and Pentecost seems far removed from our roots. Yet it marks a very necessary occasion. Jesus told his disciples that it was to their advantage for him to go away and to send them the Holy Spirit. And it isn't overstressing the point to say that without Pentecost, Christmas and Easter would have no meaning for us, for we would never have heard of them.

Strangely enough, this third great festival of the church is the oldest of the three. Its roots are in the world of the Old Testament. Israel celebrated Pentecost long before the time of Christ. It marked fifty days after the first fruits of the harvest had been gathered and was celebrated as the feast of the weeks. During this time bread was made from freshly harvested grain and offered as a sacrifice to God. Exodus 34:22ff., Leviticus 23:15-17 and Deuteronomy 16:9-12 describe this celebration.

Later on Pentecost in the Jewish religion became associated with the giving of the law to Moses on Mount Sinai. Thus it formed a parallel to our Christian celebration—Moses gave the law to his people and founded the Jewish church versus Jesus gave the Holy Spirit to the Apostles and founded the Christian church. We cannot be sure that this second meaning was already articulated by the time of Christ but the parallel is interesting.

And when is Pentecost? Because Easter jumps around on the calendar in obedience to the full moon, Pentecost can occur any time from May 10 to June 13 since it is always fifty days after Easter. Unfortunately at times Pentecost coincides with Mother's Day or the Memorial Day weekend and in some churches is further obscured by these secular holidays. Also because Trinity Sunday occurs the next week, Pentecost doesn't get the kind of celebration that Easter and Christmas do.

In some circles, particularly those that are English in background, Pentecost is called Whitsunday or White Sunday, which refers to the practice of baptizing new members on this day. The white robes worn by the candidates for Baptism gave the Sunday its name.

As mentioned previously, Pentecost marks the beginning of the non-festival half of the church year. The church calendar, like Topsy, just "growed" but perhaps by coincidence the three great festivals and most of the minor ones fall in the first half of the year. We have come to think of Christmas as occurring at the end of the year but this isn't true as far as church life is concerned. The Christian year begins with the Advent Season, four Sundays before December 25. So Epiphany, Ash Wednesday, Good Friday, Easter and Ascension Day all occur in approximately a six month period and Pentecost marks the transition to the so-called non-festival part of the calendar.

9

Only Trinity Sunday and a few Lesser Festivals are listed between Pentecost and Advent.

For a long time there was division in the church as to how these non-festival Sundays should be designated. For some reason the Protestant half of Christendom numbered the Sundays from Trinity Sunday while the Roman Catholic countries listed these days as Sundays following Pentecost. Fortunately in the recent reform of the selections to be read in church each Sunday the Protestants have agreed to number from Pentecost which brings about that much agreement and affords Pentecost a little more honor as the third of the major festivals.

Pentecost will never rival Christmas or Easter any more than the Holy Spirit will crowd Jesus out of the spotlight of Christianity. Our motto still is "Jesus is Lord," and the Holy Spirit is important to us because he brings us to Christ. But Pentecost deserves wider emphasis in the church. The days of Pentecost are important. Perhaps the hymn by William Henry Gladstone sums up best the feeling which we should have for Pentecost.

> Spirit of mercy, truth and love,
> O shed thine influence from above,
> And still from age to age convey
> The wonders of this sacred day.
>
> Unfailing Comfort, heavenly Guide,
> Still o'er thy Holy Church preside;
> Still let mankind thy blessings prove,
> Spirit of mercy, truth, and love.

*(SBH, 118)*

# Something Happened that Day

When you sit down to read the Bible, it seems like a tremendously big book. But when you concentrate on a single story, you wish the writer hadn't been so brief and so stingy with the facts. You want to say, "Wait a minute. Run through that again. Explain some of the material a little more." But the writer tells us what we need to know and then moves on to the next event or message. And there is no better example of this technique than the story of that first Pentecost.

What happened? We are overwhelmed by the noise of a rushing wind, the flickering of tongues of flame and the babel of voices. We would like to ask a dozen questions but the whole story is told in thirteen short verses. However, while we may feel a bit bewildered by Luke's account, *something important happened that day.* Don't overlook that. Before the day was over about three thousand new recruits were added to that first group of Christians. Three thousand converts as the result of one sermon preached by a former fisherman! Moreover the disciples who had previously acted like scared rabbits now had become brave as lions. In the very city where Jesus had been murdered his followers now testified in his name and defied the authorities. Something happened on Pentecost. And that something changed the whole history of the world.

The setting for the story isn't very clear. Luke tells us that they were all together in one place. Only we don't know where the place was. Somewhere in Jerusalem the eleven disciples with a few other believers waited for the promised coming of the Holy Spirit. They waited for this event because Jesus had told them to do so. For ten days they waited. And waited. And waited.

Luke says they devoted themselves to prayer. But I imagine that impulsive, impatient man, Simon Peter, also did some pacing of the floor. And the sceptical one, Thomas, probably wondered whether any good would come out of it at last. Perhaps there were times when the whole group simply sat and looked at each other. Theodore P. Ferris puts their dilemma in a nutshell when he writes:

> There are times when the hardest thing in the world is to do nothing, yet there are times when that is the only thing to do. There are some things we can work for; there are other things we can only wait for. We can work for a living; we can only wait for the spring (*The Interpreter's Bible*, Vol. 9, p. 27).

Suddenly it is the time, the proper time, and the waiting is over. God is going to make his presence felt in the world and this time he will not speak in a still small voice as he did to Elijah. The whole house where the disciples were is filled with sound, like the rushing of a mighty wind. God has no secrets anymore. The gospel is about to be proclaimed and it is as if trumpets are being blown to let the whole world know that something important is going to happen.

And now we are told that flames or tongues of fire appeared, resting on each of the disciples. We have been told before in the Bible that God's Word is like fire and here the imagery is used again. The divided flames indicate that each one is a participant in the events that follow, and in the work of spreading the gospel. Unfortunately, for our curiosity, the Book of Acts tells us little about the missionary work of most of the apostles but each one did receive the sign of the Holy Spirit at Pentecost. I suppose the men were so caught up in the excitement of the moment that they had no time to look at one another and to wonder at their strange appearance. Did they compare notes afterward? How long did it take for the fierce excitement to wear off? We shall never know, but undoubtedly Pentecost was a great moment for the disciples, who had seen so many wonders during the ministry of Jesus.

And now comes the strangest part of all. The disciples were Galileans. They couldn't even speak the language of their time, Aramaic, without an accent that caused other Jews to deride them. Yet now these Galileans began to speak in languages that they never had studied or learned. Speaking in tongues is a phenomena that has appeared many times in the history of the church. There are examples of ecstatic utterances among groups that are not Christians at all. Many authorities think that the tongues at Pentecost are simply another example of the events recorded later in Acts and mentioned by Paul in his letters to the church at Corinth. But no tongues of flame appeared in the other stories. No one elsewhere in the New Testament is mentioned as recognizing the language spoken. We must accept Luke's words or reject them. It is silly simply to try to downgrade them to a lower level of spirit manifestation.

It is strange how rumors spread in a big city. You don't need to blow sirens or flash bulletins on a TV screen in order to draw a crowd. News of a fire or a riot spreads quickly. And Pentecost seems to have been a little of both. Can't you see the streets of Jerusalem filled with hurrying spectators, all rushing to the place where the disciples were? Luke doesn't mention that any small boys or women were in the crowd but they were undoubtedly present, pushing through the crowds, seeking to get closer, demanding to know what was happening. We don't know the size of the mob but there were at least three thousand men present and probably many more than that.

Noise! It must have been deafening. There were at least twelve people talking in different tongues and some have thought the whole company of about one hundred twenty were involved in Pentecost and that would just have magnified the noise. And no crowd of three thousand would be silent. The Christian church today is sometimes overwhelmed with dignity and decorum but it didn't start that way. The scene was so wild that some spectators thought the whole thing was just a drunken brawl. Even those who were amazed to hear the gospel spoken in their native language kept asking, "What does this mean?" and that didn't contribute to quietness either.

Don't overlook those scoffers. They explained the whole business by declaring: "They are filled with new wine." In other words, the disciples were simply drunk. Peter refutes their libel by asserting that it was too early in the morning for people to be drunk, although that argument probably didn't convince the scoffers. For there are always people around to sneer at anything they cannot understand. His opponents said Jesus cast out devils by the power of the prince of demons. Festus accused Paul of having studied so much that he had gone mad. The great saints of the church have always been criticized by lesser men. Even in fields other than religion, such as science, invention, the arts, the scoffers have been busy. They were present at Pentecost and they will be with us until the end of time.

But despite the scoffers, something important happened on that first Pentecost. Three thousand people were saved, and perhaps more important, for the first time the followers of Jesus were acting for themselves. Jesus was no longer visibly present with them. The Spirit had come to guide them. But they were on their own now, no longer followers but leaders. Before this they had stood under the shadow of Jesus. They had been disciples, learning and observing. Now that time was over. The work of establishing the church of Jesus Christ in the world had begun. Three thousand people was a drop in the bucket but at least it was a beginning. To change the figure, Pentecost lit a fire that is still burning in the world today.

People love to imagine what it would have been like to have lived in the past. Every Christian probably agrees with the poet who wrote

> I think when I read that sweet story of old,
> When Jesus was here among men,
> How he called little children as lambs to his fold,
> I should like to have been with them then.

To have heard the voice of Jesus—what a thrill. But Pentecost would also have been a day to see and to hear. Out of the noise and confusion of that day the age of the Spirit began. We may find it hard to visualize the sequence of events on Pentecost but we know—something important happened that day.

# Names and Symbols

The minister was in the pulpit, preaching his sermon about the events of Pentecost. During his discourse he mentioned "the coming of the Holy Ghost." Whereupon his small son, who had probably seen too many TV programs, leaned over and whispered to his mother: "Is he a friendly ghost?" The story is a true one and indicates the problem we have when we speak of the third person of the Trinity. The word "ghost," an Anglo-Saxon word, has become so associated with peculiar psychic manifestations in haunted houses that it has been largely superseded by "spirit" which is Latin in origin. Most people today speak about the Holy Spirit, not the Holy Ghost, although the word "ghost" is still used in the Apostles' Creed.

But changing the translation to "spirit" doesn't solve all our problems. What kind of a picture does "spirit" conjure up for you? The desk dictionary I use lists fourteen definitions of spirit. None is too helpful but the one that comes the closest is: "In the abstract, life or consciousness viewed as an independent type of existence." That will not explain the word very clearly, and adding the adjective "holy" doesn't help much either. The difficulty is that we are creatures of this world, dependent on our five senses for most of our impressions and the word "spirit" doesn't involve any of them.

The Bible does use a great many different names to describe the one who descended on the disciples at Pentecost. One of the most interesting is employed by Jesus when he promised his followers that the Father would send the Holy Spirit to aid them in their work. John 14:15. The King James translation calls the coming one "the Comforter," which makes the Holy Spirit a security blanket like the one used by Linus in the Peanuts cartoons. The Revised Standard Version translates the same Greek word as "Counselor" which reminds you of a legal aid, and the New English Bible and several others stress the same idea by calling the Spirit "the Advocate." The American Bible Society translation following several earlier versions uses the term "Helper" while J. B. Phillips avoids the whole problem by calling the Holy Spirit "the one who is coming to stand by you." Each translator is trying to tell us something of what the Holy Spirit does or is by the term chosen.

There are many other names used in the Bible for the third person of the Trinity. In fact, Herbert Lockyer, in his book *All the Divine Names and Titles in the Bible* lists thirty-nine different designations in the New Testament alone. Often the Spirit is called the Spirit of God or the Spirit of Christ, which reminds us of the unity of the Trinity. At times the names used apply to the *work* of the Spirit, such as "The Spirit of Wisdom," "the Spirit of Truth," "the Spirit of Understanding." While all the names help, they do not succeed in making the Holy Spirit as plain and understandable to us as the Father or the Son.

Human beings have used symbols as well as names to describe spiritual matters. Thus the Trinity is often represented by a triangle or by interlocking circles. The cross can convey the message of the atonement, and a hand reaching down from heaven speaks of God the Father caring for his children. The Holy Spirit has been presented in symbols too in order to make his nature and work plainer to puzzled Christians.

By a strange coincidence the word for *spirit* and for *wind* is the same in both the Hebrew and the Greek language, the two major languages of the Bible. The connection between wind and spirit was picked up by Jesus when he talked to the Jewish ruler, Nicodemus, as recorded in John 3:8.

> The wind blows where it wills, and you hear the sound of it, but you do not know whence it comes or whither it goes; so it is with everyone who is born of the Spirit.

The same connection appears at Pentecost when we are told that there was a sound "like the rush of a mighty wind and it filled all the house where they were sitting." So the wind becomes a meaningful symbol of the Holy Spirit. The difficulty is that you cannot draw a picture of the wind, you cannot portray it on a banner or a pulpit hanging. As the old poem says,

> Who has seen the wind?
> Neither you nor I,
> But when the trees bow down their heads
> The wind is passing by.

19

A more tangible symbol is the dove. The figure comes from the story of Jesus' baptism where at that event Jesus saw "the Spirit of God, descending like a dove and alighting on him." Of course the dove appears in the Bible long before Jesus' baptism. Noah sent out the dove from the ark to see if the waters of the flood had subsided and when the bird didn't return, Noah knew that the earth was habitable again. In the Old Testament the dove was the only bird that could be used for sacrifice, and then only by those too poor to bring the regular animal sacrifices. It is interesting to note that Jesus' parents offered two turtledoves for him and his mother according to the law of purification. Later Jesus used the dove as a symbol of innocence when he sent his disciples out on a missionary journey and told them to be as wise as serpents and as innocent as doves (Matthew 10:16).

So the dove is a good symbol of the Spirit. The bird is quiet and unobtrusive. It soars in the heavens and lights wherever it chooses. The dove appears in church windows, on hangings and banners and is sometimes painted over the baptismal font. In an effort to portray the Spirit coming to earth from heaven, the dove is sometimes pictured as a heavenly dive-bomber hurtling toward earth. This seems to contradict the nature of both dove and Spirit but the symbol itself is otherwise meaningful.

Those tongues-like-fire, which appeared at Pentecost, added another symbol for the Holy Spirit, the symbol of fire or burning. Fire, like wind, is an ancient symbol and the connection between fire and the Holy Spirit is taken up again in the Book of Revelation where John sees seven torches or lamps "which are the Seven Spirits of God." The number *seven* often represents heaven and earth or completeness in the Bible and Christians have generally accepted this vision of seven lamps as a description of the Holy Spirit. So a flame, tongues of fire, a seven-branched candelabra or seven burning lamps all serve as meaningful symbols of the Spirit.

Fire is a good symbol for the Spirit of God. Fire gives light. Fire purifies. It provides heat and power for human beings. It can even destroy when necessary. And all those characteristics also fit the nature of the Spirit. The fire that began to burn at Pentecost is still aglow in the world. We still talk about people being "on fire with the gospel." We still want people to get "fired up for the Lord." So the flame fits, for it is the Holy Spirit we need when our enthusiasm wanes and burns low.

Yet despite the multiplicity of names and symbols the Bible gives us, the Holy Spirit remains a bit more shadowy than the other members of the Trinity. This is understandable for the work of the Spirit is centered in the human heart. As Luther reminds us in the *Small Catechism:*

> The Holy Spirit has called me through the Gospel, enlightened me with his gifts, and sanctified and kept me in the true faith. In the same way he calls, gathers, enlightens, and sanctifies the whole Christian church on earth, and keeps it united with Jesus Christ in the one true faith. In this Christian church day after day he fully forgives my sins and the sins of all believers.

That is supremely important work but it isn't work that is demonstrated by loud outward acts. Pentecost was an exception but in the days that followed that display, the Spirit continues to probe, guide and help all who will accept his aid. He will always be a bit mysterious, a bit hard to describe. But to the anxious little boy whose question appears in the first paragraph of this chapter we can answer: "Yes, he is a friendly Ghost, a friendly Spirit."

# The Language Pill

Have you ever tried to communicate with someone who doesn't speak English? That can be a frus-
trating experience. A few ideas can be expressed by
signs and motions but most thoughts are too sophis-
ticated to be transmitted by mere signs. Some people
seem to think if they shout, others will understand
a strange language even if they can't comprehend
what is spoken in an ordinary tone of voice. But all
such efforts are doomed to failure. You end up wish-
ing someone would invent a language pill that could
be popped into the mouth and give you the ability
to speak in another tongue.

The apostles on Pentecost seemed to have such a
language pill. Although they were all Galileans, Luke
tells how those first Christians "began to speak in
other tongues, as the Spirit gave them utterance."
And this wasn't mere gibberish. The writer of Acts
gives us a long list of people, "devout men from
every nation under heaven," who hear the speakers
"telling in our own tongues the mighty works of
God." Some have thought that the list of people involved, Parthians, Medes, Elamites, etc. are intended to represent the entire known world of that day

while others feel that these are the language groups of antiquity. We can't be sure, but the gospel was certainly proclaimed in many ways on that first Pentecost. The Holy Spirit seemed to function like a language pill.

Critics have said that all this was unnecessary for these Jews from various parts of the world could all understand Hebrew or Aramaic, or, failing that, they would know Greek, the common tongue of the ancient world. The objection is true for they all understood Peter when he preached to them, probably in Aramaic. But such a criticism misses the whole point of the Pentecost experience. Pentecost said to the world that the exclusiveness of the Jew was at an end. Worship of the true God would no longer be limited to a small group of Jews. Now the message is to go out to all people, people speaking the various languages used in the world.

Jesus had tried to make that plain while he was here. In the "gospel in miniature," John 3:16 we are told that God loved the *world* and that the invitation to believe is given to *whosoever*. Later on in the same Gospel Jesus tells his disciples that he has other sheep that are not of "this fold" but they are to be included in "one flock" in the future. The great commission in Matthew 28 instructs the disciples to make "disciples of all nations," and similar instructions were given just before the Ascension when Jesus tells his followers they are to be witnesses "in Jerusalem and in all Judea and Samaria and to the end of the earth."

All this is summarized in the experience at Pentecost. Perhaps the "language pill" was for the benefit of the disciples more than it was for the hearers that day. At the very outset the church gets its marching orders—everyone is to have a chance to hear the gospel, regardless of where they live or what language they speak. This seems very obvious for us today but we must remember that this was a hard thing for people of the first century to understand. For so long it had been Jews versus Gentiles. The Jews did not even enter a Gentile home. There were some proselytes in that Pentecost crowd but they had been accepted only after they had become Jews. The idea that people everywhere should have a chance to hear and accept the gospel was a hard one to understand.

Simon Peter is a good example of the problem. He had heard Jesus' words on the subject. He participated in the Pentecost experience. Yet he had to have a vision from heaven and another manifestation of the Holy Spirit before he was ready to receive the Roman, Cornelius, into the church and was willing to say, "Truly I perceive that God shows no partiality, but in every nation anyone who fears him and does what is right is acceptable to him" (Acts 10:35). Similarly it took persecution of the church to get the first Christians out of Jerusalem and into the countryside, thus spreading the gospel among the people of Judea and Samaria. And it took a church council to settle once and for all that the gospel was not to be the exclusive property of one group of people.

In some ways it was the Apostle Paul, who wasn't present on Pentecost, who caught the true meaning of that great day. For Paul carried the message of the gospel to all parts of the empire and had the courage to turn to the Gentiles when the Jews opposed him. One of the greatest declarations ever made by a human being is contained in Paul's letter to the Galatians: "There is neither Jew nor Greek, there is neither slave nor free, there is neither male nor female; for you are all one in Christ Jesus" (Galatians 3:28). Those words signaled the breakdown of the old divisions, they indicated that neither language nor race made any difference in God's sight.

Yet we cannot sit in judgment on those first Christians. Ethnic and linguistic barriers still exist among twentieth-century Christians. Some denominations still limit their major appeals to individuals of a special background or social class. Not long ago a Lutheran missionary from New Guinea told of her amusing experience with a German Lutheran in Australia. The Australian was a liberal supporter of mission work but insisted one day that Lutheranism was only for Germans. No one else could really understand this faith. The missionary asked: "Why do you give money for our New Guinea mission work?" and the man suddenly realized that the brown skinned natives in the church were also Lutherans. How narrow our thinking is at times.

Some Christians even question the need of foreign missions today. They declare: "The people in other lands have a religion. Why not let them alone?" Such people need to reread the story of Pentecost. For if the disciples hadn't finally gotten the idea of spreading the gospel to all people, regardless of race or language, most of us would still be worshiping some heathen idol or perhaps would have no religion at all.

Of course Pentecost did not abolish the barrier of language between human beings. The people of the world are still divided by the way they speak. Listen to a session of the United Nations and you will realize how difficult it still is for human beings to communicate with one another. Today there are about three thousand living languages in use and more than one hundred of these languages have at least a million people who speak this particular tongue. The various languages still make it hard to present the gospel to all nations for the Bible must be translated into each language and missionaries must spend weary times learning the correct way to speak each tongue. A language pill would be a marvelous blessing, for Pentecost didn't abolish the division of society into various groups, as described in Genesis 11, the story of the Tower of Babel. There are many times when all of us wish the whole world could learn and use a common style of speech.

Yet we must not misunderstand what happened at Pentecost. The Spirit was not telling people that it is wrong for different nations and different languages to exist. The gospel is not intended to be a leveller, forcing all people into one mold. Paul didn't mean to tell the Galatians that Jews became Gentiles or Gentiles Jews when they became Christians any more than males ceased to be males and females females when they are saved. Note that in the picture of the saved in Revelation, chapter 7 there are people "from every nation, from all tribes and peoples and tongues" gathered before the throne of God. They did not lose their identity when they became believers.

Many people like to think that their language is the original tongue from which all others are derived. The Jews believed that Hebrew was the first language. The Germans have a joke about the woman who insisted that God spoke German because according to her Bible God said to Adam, "Adam, wo bist du?" The Gaelic speakers of Scotland insist that theirs is the language of Paradise. The truth of the matter is that God likes diversity. That appears everywhere in his creation. And the different races and languages on the earth have proved a source of enrichment when we allow the various groups to exhibit their differences and their unity. Language can be a special blessing when we allow the writers and poets of a people to use the skills of their words to convey God's truth. A young Chinese girl once told a friend: "I wish you could read the Bible in Chinese. It's so beautiful in my language." No doubt she was right, but every language has its own way of conveying the message of the gospel.

Several years ago three representatives from churches in Russia came to visit students and professors at seminaries in America. One church leader, a representative of the Orthodox faith, spoke only in Russian. The second, a Roman Catholic, could converse in Latin. The third, a Lutheran, addressed the students in German. An interpreter was provided for each person but the audience really didn't feel the need of an interpreter, for they felt bound by a common Lord and one Holy Spirit guiding Christians together. There was no need for a language pill, for all were one in Christ.

That first Pentecost may have sounded like the Tower of Babel all over again. But really the situation was reversed. At the Tower of Babel human beings were driven apart by the appearance of many languages. At Pentecost people were drawn together despite the many tongues, for the witness was the same in every case. God wants all people in his kingdom.

# Plays at Pentecost

Pentecost has never inspired any particular customs for celebration. There is nothing to correspond to Christmas trees, Easter eggs, the fasting in Lent, none of the religious or secular practices that have characterized other seasons of the church year. Generally Pentecost happens, is noted, and then forgotten.

A few practices in the Middle Ages are worth mentioning. In some churches the congregation was showered with roses from the rafters on Pentecost to symbolize the tongues of flame. In other places doves were let down from the roof and released to flutter around the heads of the congregation. It is doubtful whether such a display met with universal approval. Anyone who has ever tried to get a bird out of a church building will know the problems such a practice would create. Sometimes the rushing wind of Pentecost was symbolized by the use of loud trumpets during the service. And in England the church wardens were permitted to sell a particularly potent drink called Whitsun ale to the church members on Pentecost. The money gained from this was used to repair the church and to help the poor. No doubt someone thought there was a connection between the Spirit and the potent spirits of the ale.

It was also in England that the most significant custom in connection with the season of Pentecost flourished and remains as a rich legacy for the church. This is the medieval church drama. Christian leaders when they came into power in the Roman Empire banned all plays and public entertainments on the grounds that the plays were immoral and so were the players. The accusation was probably correct in both cases. The ancient plays were filled with scenes portraying the pagan gods and goddesses. And the players were recruited from the lowest level of society. So the attack by the church was probably justified but it meant that for a period of six to seven hundred years there was no drama at all in Christendom, at least there was no formal presentation of plays.

But the dramatic instinct in human beings cannot be completely destroyed. And so drama crept back into medieval society, having its new beginning, strangely enough, in the church. Some unsung and unknown hero got the idea of brightening up the Easter service by having three monks, portraying the three Marys come to the front of the church and enquire of a fourth monk, representing the angel, where Jesus' body had been taken. The fourth character of course informed them that Jesus had risen. This little byplay, in Latin, was the beginning of the revival of drama.

Soon other biblical scenes were added, such as the shepherds coming to the manger, the temptation of Eve, Abraham offering Isaac as a sacrifice, etc. No one today can trace this growth accurately but the plays were expanded until there was an elaborate cycle from creation to the second coming. Most of the nations of Western Europe took part in this surge of drama but England took it up most enthusiastically and evolved the most striking series of plays. At first the drama was presented in the church, where the chancel provided a ready-made stage. Then the plays were moved to the steps outside and finally when the trade guilds took them over, the presentations were given in lumbering "pageant" wagons which were portable stages with an area below stage for changing costumes. These wagons were moved from place to place in the town so that you could stand in one place and eventually see the entire series of dramas or you could run from stop to stop and see one play over and over again.

Now how does Pentecost get into the act? Originally the plays were presented at the appropriate time in the church year but when the whole cycle had evolved, players began to present the dramas in a continual sequence. Corpus Christi which falls on the Thursday after Trinity Sunday was the favored time and often the plays are called Corpus Christi plays. But Corpus Christi involved a rather solemn procession through the city streets, with priests and altar boys carrying the host, the communion wafer in the procession. To follow this solemnity with a mad rush for places to see the plays, and particularly when some of the plays had come to contain rough horseplay and ribald elements caused offense, and so some cities, notably Chester in northwest England shifted the plays to the days following Whitsun Day. Thus the celebration of the coming of the Holy Spirit was followed by religious plays that chronicled the entire story of the Bible. This was a rather happy sequence.

Nothing continues forever, of course, and the plays, which had grown more secular over the years were suppressed by the Puritans when they came to power in the seventeenth century. After the restoration of Charles II to the English throne, drama became almost entirely worldly and the old religious emphasis was lost. This was a great pity and in recent years these old plays have been revived and have stirred much interest again. York, Chester, and Coventry have regular scheduled performances and draw great crowds from England and abroad.

No one knows who wrote these early plays; probably various individuals added lines from time to time. The dramas are a curious mixture of naivete and sophistication. The biblical material has a contemporary gloss and the historical situation is overlooked. Just as the painters in Italy made Jesus' mother an Italian woman of the Middle Ages, so the plays portray biblical events as if they were happening in medieval times. Thus the shepherds in the story of the birth of Jesus complain about the way they are treated by the gentry. One of the shepherds says,

> We're so burdened and tanned,
> Overtaxed and unmanned,
> We're made tame to the hand
>   Of these gentlery men.

Again the herald who announces the presence of King Herod in the play about the coming of the Wise Men calls out:

> Peace, lord barons of great renown,
> Peace, seigneur knights of noble order
> Peace, gentlemen companions of eminence,
> I command all of you keep silence.
> *(The Second Shepherd's Play)*

It is doubtful that Herod had barons and knights but that fact didn't worry the writer or the actors.

There is no sense of time as we know it. The plays are full of anachronisms. Clocks sound in the biblical plays, although the clock had not yet been invented. New Testament ideas are tossed back into the world of the Old Testament. King David performs a miracle of healing with the words: "In the name of the Father, Son and Holy Ghost, each of you shall now be whole." One of the shepherds crosses himself and says, "Pontio Pilato! Christ's cross me speed."

The crudity of the plays is further indicated by the inclusion of some horseplay to please the spectators. In an Old Testament play, Noah's wife refuses to enter the ark unless she can bring her friends along. When her sons pull her on board she boxes Noah's ear, which causes him to exclaim: "Aha! marry, this is hot!" In the New Testament plays Joseph, Pilate and Herod are also made comic figures. And the Devil, red tights and all, comes out of the bottom of the pageant wagon and runs amok among the spectators. We can understand the reason for this buffoonery but it doesn't prove very uplifting.

And yet there is a deeper level to these Corpus Christi or Whitsun plays. The writers caught some of the emotions of the biblical story. This is particularly true in the drama of Abraham and Isaac where every word that Isaac utters has terrible meaning to Abraham and reminds him of the sacrifice he is about to make. The drama reaches its climax when Isaac says,

> I would to God my mother were on this hill;
> She would plead for me on both her knees,
>     To save my life.

But since my mother is not here,
I pray you, father, change your cheer
    And kill me not with your knife.

The author also knew the meaning of this Old Testament story for at the end the Angel speaks to the congregation:

Good Christian people, these that ye have seen
    Are foreshadowers of Jesu's sacrifice,
Bearing the woes of earth most keen,
    Without gainsaying, in God's service.
So Christians all that sorrow borne
    And kept God's word without a miss,
Jesu, that wore the crown of thorn,
    Bring them all to heaven's bliss.

*(The Sacrifice of Isaac)*

It is difficult to revive old customs. But these ancient plays remind us that people remember what they see and are even more aware of what they take part in. There has been a revival of church drama in recent years and many parishioners have helped to present the message of the gospel through plays. Perhaps the ancient custom of using drama at Pentecost can provide direction to us in this modern day.

34

# Three Cheers for the Trinity

There are people who like religion to be rational, scientific, easily explainable. They want to be able to understand every teaching before they accept it. Some even make experience the measure of their belief. "I only believe what I can touch and taste and see."

Such people will never find Christianity to their liking. For no matter how carefully we word Christian doctrine, no matter how rationally we explain every teaching, there is one place where the human mind won't penetrate. The doctrine of the Trinity simply won't fit into our narrow human logic. Listen to a section from the Athanasian Creed:

> For the Father is one person, the Son is another, and the Spirit is still another.
> But the deity of the Father, Son, and Holy Spirit is one, equal in glory, coeternal in majesty.
> What the Father is, the Son is, and so is the Holy Spirit.
> Uncreated is the Father; uncreated is the Son; uncreated is the Spirit.

The Father is infinite; the Son is infinite; the Holy Spirit is infinite.

Eternal is the Father; eternal is the Son; eternal is the Spirit:

And yet there are not three eternal beings, but one who is eternal;

as there are not three uncreated and unlimited beings, but one who is uncreated and unlimited.

The mind reels. The words of the creed are biblically based. We know what the writer is saying and yet the sentences cannot be grasped rationally. The truth is beyond us. We are tempted to wonder why the church ever constructed such a doctrinal statement. Was the early church intent on creating a mystery or trying to make it a little harder for people to become Christians?

James Stewart provides the answer to this in his book *The Strong Name* (p. 251). He writes:

It (the doctrine of the Trinity) all began in the New Testament. It began in the experience of the post-Pentecost Church. It began quite simply and intuitively and untheologically. It began when men made this discovery—that they could not say all they meant by the word 'God' until they had said Father, Son, Spirit.

In other words, Stewart is saying that the idea of the Trinity was forced on those who wrote the Bible. Remember that they were Jews. And the Jew had been told until he must have become tired of hearing it that God was one. The prophets of the Old Testament spent most of their time fighting against the idea that there was more than one God. "Hear, O Israel: The Lord our God is one Lord." That was the message which was dinned into Jewish ears to keep people away from the gods of the pagans.

Those who wrote the New Testament weren't anxious to change that concept. The Apostles who began their preaching at Pentecost were not eager to put a barrier between themselves and their potential audience. But they couldn't reason away the claims that Jesus had made for himself. They couldn't rid themselves of the impression that when they had been with the Christ they had been in the presence of God himself. They had heard him tell Philip: "He who has seen me has seen the Father. . . . Do you not believe that I am in the Father and the Father in me?" (John 14:9, 10). Moreover the apostles couldn't escape the conviction that somehow the Spirit of God not only lived in heaven but lived in them as well. Somehow there was one God, and yet they knew God through three distinct persons. So the church finally accepted the doctrine of the Trinity. It wasn't a reasonable doctrine. It wasn't logical. But it was true.

The idea of having a special Sunday to celebrate the triune nature of God didn't arise until late in the history of the church. Early festivals, with the exception of Pentecost, only celebrated events in the life of Christ. Doctrinal festivals arose later. So it was not until the tenth century that a special service for the Festival of the Trinity arose in the Western Church. Bishop Stephen of Liege was apparently the author of a mass for the office of the Holy Trinity and other churches adopted this service. The practice did not immediately meet with universal acceptance, however. Pope Alexander II actually opposed Trinity Sunday on the grounds that the Trinity was honored every Sunday. But the celebration continued despite papal opposition and finally in 1334 Pope John XXII ordered the observance of Trinity Sunday throughout Western Christendom and this practice was continued by those Protestant churches that retained the custom of following the church year.

It is perhaps unfortunate that the date chosen for Trinity Sunday was the Sunday following Pentecost since this cuts short the celebration of the coming of the Holy Spirit. But the choice was inevitable. You could not celebrate Trinity Sunday until after the day the Holy Spirit was poured out and to wait any longer would push this special day still further into the non-festival half of the calendar.

How do we celebrate Trinity Sunday? Unfortunately ministers often present an abstract view of the Trinity and this is of no particular value to anyone. If the doctrine of the Trinity simply tells us about God's nature, that is of no interest to us. God can be Triune or quadune or whatever he wishes to be without affecting us in the least. But when we think of Trinity Sunday as gathering up the dates we have already celebrated in the church year—God sending his Son at Christmas, Jesus rising from the dead at Easter, the Holy Spirit descending to the church on Pentecost—this special day has meaning to us.

Thus we believe in the Trinity because we have experienced God as our Father, our Savior, and our Sanctifier. The Trinity is not to be thought of as some geometric figure like a triangle or a shamrock. The Trinity is God as we know him. John Donne began one of his dramatic sonnets with the words:

Batter my heart, three person'd God, for you
As yet but knock; breathe, shine and seek to mend;

That I may rise and stand, o'erthrow me, and bend
Your force, to break, blow, burn and make me new.

It is this Triune God who makes us new. It is as hard
for us to accept the Trinity as it was for those first
Christians but like them we can find no other way to
describe the God who reveals himself to us.

Trinity Sunday then is a proper part of the days
of Pentecost. It is not a time for philosophical reason-
ing or even for marveling over the mystery of God's
nature. It is a time to think of God's goodness to us,
of God's care and concern. Trinity Sunday is the
right time to sing that great song of the church:

> Holy, holy, holy, Lord God Almighty!
> Early in the morning our song shall rise to thee;
> Holy, holy, holy, merciful and mighty,
> God in three Persons, blessed Trinity.

( LBW, 165 )

# Living in the Spirit

We have done with dogma and divinity
   Easter and Whitsun past,
The long, long Sundays after Trinity
   Are with us at last;
The passionless Sundays after Trinity,
   Neither feast-day nor fast.
             *(After Trinity)*
      JOHN MEADE FALKNER

Neither feast-day nor fast. The Sundays that follow Pentecost or Trinity Sunday may seem dull for the Christian. No singing of Christmas carols. No solemn Good Friday or joyous Easter. Simply a monotonous numbering of Sundays after Pentecost until the total may reach twenty-seven before we come to "The Last Sunday after Pentecost." The non-festival half of the church year is exactly that—non-festival. Someone has said life is so daily, and in the same way church life can seem so weekly, no matter how you spell the word. But this second half of the church year is the most important one for the Christian, more important than Christmas or Easter.

For at Pentecost God says to his church, "Now

it's your turn. What difference has it made to you that I sent my Son into the world? What difference has it made that Jesus died on the cross and rose again? What difference does it make that the Holy Spirit has come to guide you?" Someone has said that Pentecost says "So what?" to the people on this earth. And our response determines the pattern of our whole life, on earth and in eternity.

Note that first Pentecost. After the crowd had seen and heard the coming of the Spirit and had listened to Peter telling them how God had sent his son and had raised him from the dead, the hearers didn't say, "Isn't that wonderful!" They didn't throw a glorious block party or organize a dance. They said to Peter and the rest of the disciples: "Brethren, what shall we do?" And after the three thousand had been baptized "they devoted themselves to the apostles' teaching and fellowship, to the breaking of bread and the prayers." They answered God's "so what?" They began to live in the Spirit.

Sometimes we think of Christianity in terms of the thief on the cross. He repented, came to faith and died. But most of us repent, come to faith and *live*. And that means facing life day after day. It means overcoming temptations, using opportunities to do good, making progress in our Christian growth. For Christianity is a day by day activity, a living in the Spirit. The days that follow Pentecost, the non-festival days, should remind us of that.

Did you ever wonder why the Bible, particularly the New Testament, contains so many statements about Christian living? After all, we are saved by grace, not works. Yet the Sermon on the Mount contains injunctions about forgiving others, short statements about the sanctity of marriage, instructions about prayer and warnings about judging others. The Epistles are full of statements about how we are to conduct ourselves toward the government and toward our neighbors. One could easily be led into the idea that we save ourselves if we weren't reminded from time to time of the great things God has done for us. But all these injunctions are simply reminders to be what we are, the children of God. The New Testament calls on us to live our lives in the Spirit and that is the message of the days of Pentecost.

Christianity has two directions and the church calendar includes both the horizontal and the vertical element of our faith. The first part of the year stresses the vertical, God reaching down to us and our responding to him by praising and thanking him. But in the days after Pentecost the stress is on the horizontal, human beings reaching out to those around them. The second chapter of the Bible says it isn't good for human beings to be alone in this world and we aren't. Life consists of relationships in marriage, business, politics, recreation, etc. Unless we live alone in some remote wilderness area, we come in contact with other people every day. It's as if God placed us on a stage with other actors and then sat in the audience to observe the action.

Fortunately it isn't quite like that. If we have to live the Christian life without any divine help, we'll make a mess of things. It is important to remember that Pentecost begins this non-festival half, for the message of Pentecost is that you are not alone. The Spirit has come and now lives in the believer's heart. Jesus told his disciples that he would be with them to the close of the age and that promise was fulfilled in the coming of the Spirit. God is not just a spectator, he is a participant in our lives for the entire year. Day by day he walks with us. We live in the Spirit.

And it is this dailiness of life that threatens us. Anyone can feel religious at Christmas or Easter. The hard part is to feel close to God on wash day, blue Monday or any day when everything goes wrong at the office or the factory. Macbeth talks about

> Tomorrow, and tomorrow, and tomorrow,
> Creeps in this petty pace from day to day
> To the last syllable of recorded time,

and we all know that feeling of day following day and life seemingly having no meaning or purpose. It is at such a time that we need to feel the presence of the Holy Spirit strengthening us and walking with us. The great battles of life are more easily won than the little struggles of existence. In Bunyan's *Pilgrim's Progress* Christian wins his great battle against the devil, called Apollyon, but almost loses his soul by wandering in a pleasant path that lies beside the true road to heaven. The days of Pentecost remind us of the importance of living each day in the Spirit.

On my desk lies a letter from a woman who is interested in the church but who is repelled by the actions of a layman she has met. The man holds a church office and assists in the distribution of communion on Sundays but he also shows overbearing pride in himself. He ignores children that ask for his help; he sits in harsh judgment over other members of the congregation. The letter ends with the words: "He could never make me believe his church is the true Christian church."

Christians bristle at such an attack. We insist that it is wrong to judge the church by the weakness of an individual. We remind others that there are hypocrites among the members and that even faithful Christians remain sinners as long as they live. But the world judges us by what the gospel produces in daily living. From the beginning of Christianity human beings were won for Christ by demonstrations of Christian love as much as they were won by the words that preachers spoke. "See how these Christians love one another," one of the early pagan writers said, and love has often been the key to open a locked human heart. "What you are speaks so loudly that I cannot hear what you say." We may not like that statement but we must recognize that it expresses the reactions of many.

So all those numbered Sundays after Pentecost are important. They are the days when the church spells out what it means to be a Christian, what it means to live in the Spirit. Christmas and Easter may be great days for the believer but what that believer does on a hot day in July or a cold day in January may be more important to someone outside the faith. Jesus told us to be salt and light in this world and we are that only when we learn to live in the Spirit.

# God's Calendar

"Cross my palm with silver, dearie, and I'll tell your fortune." Few can resist such an invitation, even when the soothsayer is dirty and ignorant. Most of us are interested in the future, even though we would probably be miserable if we knew everything that would happen to us next year or even next day. It is uncertainty that provides the spice to life.

But the future isn't just what will happen to an individual but what will occur to the world as we know it. In the face of many dire predictions, we wonder whether the human race will continue as it has in the past. Will the sun be shining a thousand years from now or will the earth be plunged into a new ice age? Will our solar system continue or end up as a black hole in space? What are our chances in this universe?

Most of us are inclined to believe that what has been will continue to be, that life will not change very much in the foreseeable future. The author of Ecclesiastes expresses the monotony and unchangeableness of existence in the following way:

> Generations come and generations go, but the world stays just the same. The sun still rises,

and it still goes down, going wearily back to where it must start all over again. The wind blows south, the wind blows north—round and round and back again. . . . Everything leads to weariness—a weariness too great for words. (Ecclesiastes 1:4-6, 8 TEV).

On the other hand, there are voices today crying "calamity, calamity" to the world. People are predicting a nuclear holocaust, a new ice age, a change in the earth's climate that will make life unlivable on this earth. Gabriel's words in *Green Pastures* seem most fitting to many: "Everything that's nailed down is coming loose."

Christians naturally turn to the Bible for help, hoping to catch there a glimpse of the future. The first glance is disappointing, for the Bible seems to spend most of its pages talking about the past. God seems to have been very active in the days of the Old Testament and again when Christ was here. But with the coming of the Holy Spirit, the great days seem to be over. One can understand the reaction of the small boy when he heard some of the Old Testament stories: "God must have been more exciting in those days." But when you study the Bible carefully you find that God's word does have something to say about the future. It becomes apparent that there are still some things left on God's calendar, some important events that have not yet taken place. The Christian church has grouped these things under the heading of "eschatology" which means "last things." Moreover the church year calendar has reserved a special time to discuss these events on God's calendar. The last Sundays after Pentecost usually feature biblical readings that have to do with the future. The final Sunday in the church year is called Christ the King and stresses Christ as the ruler of all things. This Sunday is followed by the Advent season where stress is also placed on the second coming of Christ. So let's take a look at what still remains on God's calendar.

Before we begin we must admit that the Bible does not give us a complete blueprint of the future. People who try to find references in the Bible to all the major events of human history are wasting their time. Moreover the passages that do deal with the future are difficult to interpret, for often the writer uses allegories and figures of speech to cloak the meaning. Thus Ezekiel sees strange wheels in the air and writes about a valley full of dead men's bones but doesn't explain all this. Daniel sees strange visions in the night but people are still arguing about the meaning of the visions. Jesus gives his disciples warnings about the future but it isn't always clear to us whether he is talking about the destruction of Jerusalem or the end of the world or both. And the last book of the Bible, Revelation, is full of tantalizing visions and events but Bible experts have never agreed on what the author meant. The history of the church is filled with stories of Bible students who were sure that they were living in the last days and yet they died and the world continued to exist. Martin Luther didn't think the world could last another 100 years but we have celebrated the 450th anniversary of the Reformation.

So we must approach the subject of the future with caution. After all, the people in Jesus' day thought they understood all the prophecies about the Messiah, yet they were dead wrong. So when we finish the season of Pentecost by talking about the last things, we must do so carefully. But there are some truths that seem clearly revealed through the Holy Spirit. Let's take a look at several of them.

1. There will be an end to the present world! The endless round of monotony that Ecclesiastes discusses *will* have an end. The people who talk about calamities overtaking this earth are at least in the right ball park. A few simple passages make this message clear.

> And the world passes away, and the lust of it; but he who does the will of God abides for ever (1 John 2:17).
>
> But the day of the Lord will come like a thief, and then the heavens will pass away with a loud noise, and the elements will be dissolved with fire, and the earth and the works that are upon it will be burned up (2 Peter 3:10).
>
> Then comes the end, when he delivers the kingdom to God the Father after destroying every rule and every authority and power (1 Cor. 15:24).
>
> Then I saw a new heaven and a new earth; for the first heaven and the first earth had passed away (Rev. 21:1).

It would be possible to extend that list for one of the basic truths of the Bible, particularly the New Testament, is that this present world will be replaced by a new and cleansed creation.

The Bible says a number of things about this end of the world. It warns that no one except God knows the date when this event will occur. Despite that warning, the daters have been busy trying to read God's mind almost from the day the Bible was completed. We are also told that there will be a general resurrection from the dead at the end of time, followed by the day of judgment. We are given warning signs of the end but these are general enough to keep us from saying in any age, "The end can't come now."

Some people believe all the Jews will be converted before the end. Some, on the basis of a passage in Revelation, believe that Christ will reign for a thousand years on this earth before the end comes. Recently there has been a great deal of interest in the idea of a rapture, that is, that the good people, the believers, will be snatched away from the earth and be with Christ for a period of time before the end. For many of these ideas the only answer seems to be: "We will have to wait and see." But the basic truth is clear enough to be proclaimed when we study the last things—this world will not continue forever as it is now. Abraham Lincoln once said this nation couldn't continue forever half slave and half free. He was right. The Bible says this world can't continue forever half sinful and half saved. A change is coming.

An interesting sidelight to this is provided by that peculiar passage in 2 Peter that speaks about the heavens and the earth being destroyed by fire. There was a time when many were inclined to sneer at such a statement, but since the splitting of the atom and the creation of A-bombs and H-bombs, the sneering has died down a bit. In fact, a report on Science and Human Survival presented before the American Academy for the Advancement of Scienced contained the prediction that a future nuclear war might run the risk "of ending human history altogether." A sobering thought.

2. The end of all things centers in Jesus Christ! One of the most striking scenes in the Bible occurs just before Pentecost. The disciples are with Jesus on a hill near Jerusalem when suddenly he is gone and a messenger tells the gaping disciples: "Men of Galilee, why do you stand looking into heaven? This Jesus, who was taken up from you, will come in the same way as you saw him go into heaven." Those words form a fitting close to the ministry of Jesus, for he had promised that he would return and now the promise is repeated. Connect that promise with the great events described in Revelation 11, where after an angel blows a trumpet, loud voices in heaven say, "The kingdom of the world has become the kingdom of our Lord and of his Christ, and he shall reign forever and ever."

Of course the second coming is often stressed in Advent too, but it cannot be omitted from the message at the end of the Pentecost season because Jesus is the trigger that sets off all the rest of the action. He is the bridegroom at the heavenly feast; he is the lamb in Revelation, slain for the sins of the world; he is the judge before whom the nations gather; he is the one who promises at the end of the Bible: "Surely I am coming soon" (Rev. 22:20). We are not always aware of how deeply this return motif is woven into our Christian theology and worship. Those churches that still use the Apostles' Creed in Sunday worship join each week in confessing: "From thence he (Jesus Christ) shall come to judge the quick and the dead." And as Christians continue to celebrate the sacrament of communion they are doing what Paul said: "For as often as you eat this bread and drink the cup, you proclaim the Lord's death *until he comes*" (1 Cor. 11:26).

We must admit that the doctrine of the second coming has often fallen into neglect in the church. The final Sundays of the church year have been used for other stresses and people have become too concerned about this world only and have relegated thoughts about the second coming to the area of fanaticism. Yet the situation isn't as bad as it seems, for while we may not be too conscious of the teaching itself, we all long for what it means. Every Christian longs for a world at peace, a world freed from sin and death. Every Christian would like to feel closer to Jesus than he or she does now. And all those longings are fulfilled with the return of Jesus. The great missionary hymn by Isaac Watts finds its fulfillment only when this world becomes the world that God intended it to be:

> Jesus shall reign where'er the sun
> Doth his successive journeys run;
> His kingdom stretch from shore to shore,
> Till moons shall wax and wane no more.
> (*LBW*, 530)

3. We must be ready for the end! Jesus, while he was here, was concerned that people would not be prepared for the end of things. He warned his disciples and others by figures and parables that they should be careful not to be taken by surprise. So he told them and us that he would come like a thief in the night. He told the parable of the Ten Virgins, five of whom were caught unprepared for the return of the bridegroom. He told about the foolish servants that were not attending to business when their master returned. He spoke the parable of the talents and the pounds, about a servant who simply buried his money in the ground instead of using it in prepara-

51

tion for his lord's return. Many of these warnings are read in the church during the last Sundays of the church year. Their message is clear. Keep awake. Like a good Boy Scout, be prepared.

It isn't hard to see why the Bible contains so many warnings on this subject. Even with the best of intentions we can grow careless. Life is full of so many things and as the world goes on day after day with no change occurring, it is easy to place the doctrine of last things in the "interesting but remote" file. Perhaps a story from the area of stewardship may make this clear. A man was approached by his pastor and asked for a contribution for the church. He pleaded that he owed too many bills to afford such a contribution at the moment. "But don't you think you owe the Lord something, too?" asked the pastor.

"Oh, yes," was the reply, "but he isn't pushing me like those others are." That's the difficulty with the end-time of the earth. It doesn't push at us. It simply happens. Paul warns the Christians in Thessalonica: "When people say, 'There is peace and security,' then sudden destruction will come upon them" (1 Thess. 5:3). Even the warning signs at the end are not enough to keep us from dreaming if we choose to, for the signs given by Jesus can occur at other times too.

Yet we should understand what it means to be ready. It means to be busy about the Lord's work, putting the things of God first in our life. It does not mean being obsessed with last things. A story from the early history of this country will show the proper attitude. One day in the early nineteenth century the sun suddenly was darkened, although there was no eclipse. Many people thought this was the end of the world. At that time a trial was being held in a small Kentucky town and some of the participants thought the court should recess and everyone go to the church to pray. But one of the lawyers objected, saying that if his Lord was returning, he would prefer to be found doing the business that God had called him to do in this world. That's being prepared, being ready and being diligent about your task in life.

God's calendar is undoubtedly a busy one. He has a whole universe to run. He notes even the fall of a sparrow on this earth. But undoubtedly he has a special red mark against the day when Jesus Christ will return to take charge of his people on this earth. It is only proper that we end the days of Pentecost by thinking about the last things, the events that will put an end to this sinful earth and begin the new life for all of us.

PART II

# The Christian in Summer

# That Summertime
# Feeling

Because Easter dances around on the calendar, the Pentecost season can begin anytime from May 10 to June 13. Despite this variation, it always includes that section of the secular calendar that we call summer. And summer conjures up pictures of hot, lazy weather, of vacation time, trips to faraway places and all the activities that we have come to identify with June, July, and August.

The idea of vacations hasn't always been associated with summer. In the past there has always been a leisure class that could come and go at will, but for the majority of people summer just meant working under hotter and more unpleasant conditions. Even schoolchildren didn't get vacations, they simply moved from their classes to hard manual work in the harvest fields. Summer just meant different kinds of chores.

Of course there were always holidays such as the Fourth of July. People did get a day or so of leisure, but the idea that each working person was entitled to a vacation, a period of one or more weeks to be spent as one wished, was not even dreamed of. Those who talk about the good old days will have to include in that picture a world with no vacations, no real leisure time for working people and farmers.

Today most people do receive some kind of vacation. It is written into labor contracts or guaranteed when a person begins employment. Even those who are their own bosses or who are not gainfully employed think in terms of a change of scenery when the hot summer months come along. The automobile and the airplane have made vacation trips possible and have put our population on the move.

But what about the Christian in the summertime? Are we entitled to a vacation from our faith? Do we say, "Good-bye God and church. We'll see you in the fall"? Obviously not. We are not to be part-time Christians regardless of the season of the year. Yet life *is* different in the summer. Church activity slows down. Substitutes appear in the pulpit because the pastor is out of town. Members travel to different parts of the country and of the world. Even those who stay at home need a change of pace, for God does not expect us to work all the time. Note the festival seasons that were commanded in the Old Testament. Jesus often withdrew from the people to spend time in prayer and rest, and on one occasion at least he told his disciples: "Let us go off by ourselves to some place where we will be alone and you can rest awhile" (Mark 6:31 TEV).

The church has kept pace with the emphasis on vacations and does offer special outdoor activities in the summer. Bible camps and conferences for all ages offer new horizons and opportunities for Christians to be together. Such programs can be a real source of blessing for those in attendance. Many young men and women who have volunteered for full-time service in the church trace their decision to the inspiration received at a summer Bible camp.

However, not everyone can attend a camp or conference, and such gatherings do not extend over the entire summer part of the Pentecost season. So this section of *The Days of Pentecost* is intended to suggest some activities that you can participate in during the summer months. Each of the five following chapters lists a type of recreation which you can do by yourself, with other members of the family, or with other Christians. You may be able to dream up some other activities that fit your life-style better. The important thing is that you should use the summer days of Pentecost as a time for varying your Christian life. Summer is a beautiful season. The days of June are rare, as James Russell Lowell wrote, and July and August have their appeal. The summer part of the Pentecost season should bring joy and strength to the Christian.

# The World Underfoot

A famous naturalist, accompanied by a friend from the city, once took a walk through the woods. Suddenly the naturalist stopped. "Hear that?" he asked. "It's a shrew moving among the leaves." But the city dweller couldn't hear anything in the stillness.

Later the two men walked together through the city streets. "Hear that?" said the native of the city. "Somebody dropped some money." But the naturalist heard nothing except the noise of the traffic.

Whether that's a true story or not, it points out that we hear what we are trained to hear, and similarly we see what we expect to see. Unfortunately most of us walk through life, blind to a thousand wonders. The wind rustles the leaves, birds swoop and chirp, bees hum around colorful flowers and we drive to the grocery store or the filling station, oblivious to the beauty and mystery around us. Perhaps that's inevitable in our busy world.

But summertime is a time for seeing. People travel thousands of miles to glimpse the Grand Canyon or the World Trade Building. Many take long trips by sea and air to glimpse the natives of Scotland or Hong Kong. Such experiences can be rewarding if we really observe the common bond among all people and do not conclude: "I thank thee, God, I'm not like these people." But summer can be a time to open our eyes to God's world on a smaller scale too.

This chapter is about grass, that fascinating green material that covers so much of the earth. Perhaps you think of grass as stuff that has to be mowed when you'd rather do something else, or as a fragile plant that never seems to win the battle against noxious weeds. Take another look. Grass is one of God's most wonderful creations. This world would be far different, if it could even exist at all, without grass. Sarah P. Riedman, in her book on this subject, puts the problem very well:

> Where would our world be without grass? It wouldn't be green of course. But that is not all. Your lawn would be a muddle in the rain and a dust bowl under the hot sun. No lawns, no gardens, no parks, no golf courses, no airport runs . . .

The writer goes on to remind us that without grass we would have no milk on the table and no butter for bread, since the cattle of the world are dependent on grass for sustenance.

But we will not learn much by speculating about what the world would be like if there were no grass. What we need to do is look at what does grow in our world. So I invite you to take a look at grass. Pick a nice dry day. Mark off an area about ten feet by ten feet in the park or someplace where the grass has been allowed to grow with no care except mowing. And begin to look. And look. And look.

The first thing you will observe is the tremendous variety in such a small area. Not all that you see will technically be grass, but that's a handy name for anything that grows on a lawn. You will discover short blades and long blades, frilly leaves, tiny ferns, mosses, an almost endless variety of growths. There are about 1000 kinds of grasses in the United States and more than 5000 in the world. There are more than 200,000 kinds of plants that have been classified on this earth. Genesis describes all this with the simple statement:

> Then he (God) commanded, "Let the earth produce all kinds of plants, those that bear grain and those that bear fruit," and it was done. So the earth produced all kinds of plants, and God was pleased with what he saw (Gen. 1:11-12 TEV).

Did you ever consider what a dull world this would be if there were only one or two varieties of plants on the earth? We could probably get by with a lot less than 200,000 kinds, and such a reduction in numbers might appeal to our systematic, stylized minds. But God doesn't do things that way. He makes a million snowflakes in a million different shapes and he has given us wonderful variety in a simple thing like grass. Compare the structures, the delicate shapes of many of the grasses. Even the color varies from plant to plant. An Irish song talks about *Forty Shades of Green,* and that's not an exaggeration. You can see a dozen shades in your ten-foot square. The plants all blend together and they speak of God's prodigal giving.

Now take hold of the grass and pull. You will find it doesn't come out by the roots very easily. You may think that the ground holds the grass but it really is the other way around. The grass holds the soil in place. Strip your yard of grass and soon erosion valleys will form. And dust will blow. And eventually you will have a sandy desert or a barren stretch of rock. This has happened in many places where human beings have foolishly stripped away the grass cover. For grass has an important part to play in God's world, just as you and I have. Like everything God made, grass has its place in the scheme of things. In a famous poem entitled *Grass*, Carl Sandburg pictures the green stuff busily covering up the battlefields of the world, Gettysburg, Waterloo, and others. The grass promises that eventually people will no longer recognize these places of slaughter and bloodshed. Sandburg ends with the significant words:

> I am the grass
> Let me work.

While you sit and look at that ten-foot plot of grass, something remarkable is happening before your eyes. You are witnessing a first class manufacturing concern in operation. The roots underground are drawing up water and other supplies from the soil. The plant stem is conveying this material to the leaf. And the leaf, by the wonderful process known as photosynthesis, is producing food that will go back to nurture the stem and the roots and thus keep the process going. While human beings talk about using the sun to take care of our energy needs, the grass is busy taking sustenance from the soil and the air to sustain its own life. And the grass never went to college to learn how to do that!

Jesus must have sat and looked at a plot of grass on more than one occasion. For he said, in the Sermon on the Mount:

61

And why worry about clothes? Look how the wild flowers grow; they do not work or make clothes for themselves. But I tell you that not even King Solomon with all his wealth had clothes as beautiful as one of these flowers. It is God who clothes the wild grass—grass that is here today and gone tomorrow, burned up in the oven. Won't he be all the more sure to clothe you? What little faith you have (Matt. 6:28-30 TEV).

Anyone who looks at a plot of grass for any length of time cannot help be impressed by the beauty, the structure, the design of this lowly growth. Even in a tiny blade of grass you can see the handiwork of the greate designer. Walt Whitman once wrote about grass:

I guess it is the handkerchief of the Lord,
A scented gift and remembrancer designedly dropt,
Bearing the owner's name someway in the corners,
    that we may see and remark, and say *Whose?*
                *(Song of Myself)*

Now pluck a blade of grass from the lawn. Or pull up a weed and toss it away. With that simple action a living thing has ceased to exist. Growing things are fragile things, springing up suddenly, then quickly withering away, as Jonah's gourd vine did. Jesus comments that the grass is here today and gone tomorrow and when you pull up a blade of it you are illustrating one of the favorite messages of the Bible writers. For they have seen in the fragile nature of grass a warning to all of us that we do not live forever. Isaiah 40:6-8 (TEV) contains these words:

A voice cries out, "Proclaim a message!"
"What message shall I proclaim?" I ask.

"Proclaim that all mankind are like grass;
   they last no longer than wild flowers.
Grass withers and flowers fade when the Lord
   sends the wind blowing over them.
People are no more enduring than grass.
Yes, grass withers and flowers fade,
   but the word of our God endures forever."

Peter repeats these words in his first epistle, and the message is as true today as it was in Bible times. Our ten square feet of lawn should remind us of the nature of life. We will have a longer existence than the stalk of grass that we uproot so easily, yet eventually our ending comes too. All flesh is like grass. It is significant that the grass someday may cover us.

Yet, don't get too depressed as you sit on the lawn and study nature's carpet. Flesh is like grass, but that's not all the story. Isaiah reminds us that the word of God endures forever. And that word has promised us eternal life. We are grass but we are more than grass, for we are the children of God. We may be here today and gone tomorrow but there is another day for us, a day of resurrection and reunion.

Ten square feet of grass. Look at it and study it carefully. It is a good game for a summer's day. If you wish, go to the library and get some books on the subject. You may want to try to identify the grasses and other small plants on your lawn. Some of them have fascinating names such as Job's tears, yellow foxtail, bottle brush grass, quaking grass, lady's shoes, etc. But above all, learn to look carefully at what God has made. He said the earth was good, and despite our sin it still is. Even a blade of grass can convey God's truth to us. As the poet Tennyson once said about a flower:

Flower in the crannied wall
I pluck you out of the crannies,
I hold you here, root and all, in my hand,
Little flower—but *if* I could understand
What you are, root and all, and all in all,
I should know what God and man is.

# The World Overhead

Archaeologists today are busy digging up the past. They are finding remains left by our ancestors who lived thousands of years ago. Most of the finds are carefully preserved and transferred to a museum where visitors can gaze on these relics of the past. There *is* a thrill in looking at an inscription or a piece of pottery that Abraham or David or Jesus may have seen. Yet every night that the skies are clear it is possible to see objects that Abraham and David and Jesus must have seen once upon a time. For though the stars may have shifted slightly in their relation to the earth, essentially they are the same points of light that people have seen in every age.

Thus when God took Abraham out under the night sky and said to him: "Look toward heaven, and number the stars, if you are able to number them" (Gen. 15:5), he was showing Abraham the same sky that we see now. When the psalmist wrote: "The heavens are telling the glory of God; and the firmament proclaims his handiwork" (Ps. 19:1), he was talking about the same sky that we observe. The stars are relics of the past, part of the constant background, the scenery for the stage where human life is lived.

Usually we are too busy to concern ourselves with stars. They are simply there when we walk from the house to the car. We take stars for granted, just as we do houses and streets and trees and the rest of our scenery. And for most parts of this country, star-gazing can be a cold and unpleasant occupation for much of the year. But in the summer, even the busy Christian needs to take time to look at God's heaven. Studying the world overhead can be a pleasant and profitable recreation. If you are spending vacation time at the lake or the beach or the mountains, you may have the advantage of cleaner air for night study. But even if you are at home, sitting outside enjoying a cool evening breeze, you can engage in stargazing and you don't need any equipment except your own eyes, although you can enhance your appreciation of God's universe if you have access to a telescope or even a pair of field glasses.

How do we study the world overhead? What should we look for? One way is just to sit and look in wonder at its beauty. Gerard Manley Hopkins begins one of his poems with the injunction:

> Look at the stars! look, look up at the sky!
> O look at all the fire-folk sitting in the air!
> The bright boroughs, the circle-citadels there!
>
> *(The Starlight Night)*

The exclamation marks stress the wonder and the mystery of it all. People in every age have followed Hopkins' injunction to look, and poets especially have found this an exciting occupation. You don't have to know the names of the stars, their distances from the earth, their chemical composition, nothing. You just need to look and to appreciate beauty. In a very moving scene in *The Merchant of Venice* Lorenzo tells his wife, Jessica:

> Sit, Jessica: look how the floor of heaven
> Is thick inlaid with patines of bright gold.

Everyone who takes the time to look can see those "patines of bright gold."

But just sitting and looking can also have another benefit. Stargazing can help put life into proper perspective. The cares and worries of business and of daily living seem smaller and less difficult when measured against the presence of the stars. June Dake in an article in *The Christian Herald* (July 1973) tells about a businessman who stayed home from a dinner because he was worried about many problems. When the family returned, they found him in the backyard, looking up at the sky. He told them:

> When I came out here, I thought the problem I was wrestling with at work was hopeless. But the longer I lay here looking up at all that beauty, the smaller the problem seemed. I've got it only partly worked out, but I'm sure I've got it licked.

An unknown poet once said that she lost her cares by wandering through fields by the sea. The sky at night can be an equally good place to scatter our doubts and troubles. We may not find complete relief but at least life will look different, measured against the immensity of the sky.

Yet ignorance isn't necessarily bliss when we are gazing at the stars. Our appreciation of the world overhead is greatly increased when we begin to study what scientists have learned about the stars. I'm not suggesting that you enroll in a course in astronomy, although that can be a worthwhile experience, but there are books available in almost every public library that feature popular material about the sky. If you are exploring the world overhead by yourself, you may want to read some of these books; if the family takes on stargazing as a summer project, one member might be given the task of gathering statistics and other facts about the stars.

Once you begin, you will be overwhelmed by size and numbers. Even with the naked eye we can see about three thousand stars. But when the great telescopes go into action the result is staggering. In our own galaxy there are about 100,000 million stars and there are millions of other galaxies. No one can even come close to grasping the tremendous numbers of heavenly bodies in existence. God's challenge to Abraham to number the stars is still a challenge to us today.

Equally stunning is the vastness of the universe. The millions of stars are not crowded into a small corner with standing room only. Scientists do not measure distances by miles but by light years. Everyone is familiar with that magic number, 186,000, which represents the number of miles per second that light travels through the universe. That is too fast for us to comprehend. Consider for a moment that it takes light from the nearest star about 4½ years to reach this earth. Or reckon with the fact that there are stars in our own galaxy more than 22,000 light years distant from us. The discovery that some stars seem to be more than 37 million light years away simply makes our head whirl. The wiseacre who said, why shouldn't light travel that fast, it's downhill all the way, didn't help us much.

Studying the stars can lead into all kinds of interesting side views. You may learn about quasars, black holes, double stars, comets, asteroids, and dozens of other fascinating subjects. The history of astronomy is filled with remarkable discoveries and some unpleasant examples of human pigheadedness and prejudice. Also, if there is a planetarium near your home, you should plan to visit it with the family or a group of friends. Such an experience indoors may increase your fascination with the world overhead. A summertime recreation can easily turn into a lifetime hobby.

Yet we should not forget the words of the psalmist: "The heavens are telling the glory of God; and the firmament proclaims his handiwork" (Ps. 19:1). It is in the interpretation of facts and reactions that we gain the most from stargazing. It would be unfair for me to tell you what you are supposed to see as you study God's creation. But let me list a few of the things that I find there. Perhaps you will also discover these truths and can greatly augment the list from your study of the world overhead.

1. What a great God we have. The maker is always greater than the thing which he makes, the architect must always dream the dream before he builds the house. So, if our universe is so breathtakingly beautiful and amazing, what a testimony that is to the one who called the heavens into being. Genesis 1 says it so simply—"In the beginning God created the heavens and the earth." A little later in this opening chapter we get the magnificence of the night summed up in five words: "He made the stars also." The Book of Job expands a little on this subject. Toward the end, God challenges Job and says in part:

> Can you tie the Pleiades together
>> or loosen the bonds that hold Orion?
> Can you guide the stars season by season
>> and direct the Big and the Little Dipper?
> Do you know the laws that govern the skies,
>> and can you make them apply to the earth?
>
> (Job 38:31-33 TEV)

But modern science as it has probed the universe has unwittingly given us a grander picture of God than people have had in the past. A bit of stargazing can convince us that J. B. Phillips was right when he titled a book *Your God Is Too Small.* The sense of awe and reverence which is characteristic of the Old Testament should also be a part of our faith as we think about the greatness of the Creator. It has been said that the way to cure a man of atheism is to make him study the stars for six months. That method won't necessarily work, for some have eyes and see not. But the Christian who learns about the world overhead should have a deeper appreciation of God.

2. What a great Savior we have. A number of years ago I wrote a play about the coming of the Son of God to this earth. One of the angels protested that the Son should not waste his time trying to save human beings.

> There are millions of worlds in the universe, and if there aren't enough, he can always make more. It isn't fair for him to waste time on one little world like that. (*Let Us Adore Him,* p. 71)

We might all feel that way when we consider how great this universe is. This earth is hardly a speck of dust in the cosmos. We aren't even the largest planet in our solar system and our sun is not the center of the galaxy.

Yet the Son of God was born in a manger in Bethlehem and died on a cross on Calvary so that we might be saved from our sins. What an impression of love! How easy it would have been to have written this world off as a failure. But God didn't do that. He sent his Son to save us. One of the most striking examples of this care occurred when Jesus cried from the cross: "I thirst." Think of it. The Lord of the universe lacked a cup of water because he came to save me. In the words of Isaac Watts:

> Amazing pity, grace unknown
> And love beyond degree.

3. The need for a personal God. There was a day when people worshiped the sun, moon and stars, and that was very foolish. For the objects in the world overhead go on their way unheeding, unconcerned. The stars are out, night after night, but they show no concern for me as an individual. If I am happy, they shine. If I am sad, they are still in their places, millions of miles away and totally unaffected by my condition. As *The Rubaiyat* puts it:

And that inverted Bowl they call the Sky
Whereunder crawling coop'd we live and die,
   Lif not your hands to *It* for help, for It
As impotently moves as you or I.

The glory of our Christian faith is that we have a personal, caring God, made even more personal by the coming of the Son to this earth. We can understand the remark of the little girl who was afraid of the dark. When she was told that God would be with her, she whimpered, "But I want someone with a face." We do have someone with a face, human, loving, concerned. The marvels of the world overhead are no substitute for a God who cares for us, lives in our heart and hears us when we pray.

Now you take it from there. Gaze at the stars on a warm summer night. Revel in their beauty. Learn about their wonders. See what the world overhead tells you about God. Stargazing can be a pleasant occupation for a few nights—or a source of interest and joy for the rest of your life.

# An Adventure
# in Architecture

"But it doesn't look like a church!" Those words were probably spoken in London when Christopher Wren rebuilt St. Paul's Cathedral after the disastrous fire of 1666. Accustomed to Gothic structures, the people must have found the pillared porch and the great central dome very strange. But in an earlier age, Giorgio Vasari, a critic, historian and architect, called the developing Gothic style "monstrous and barbarous, an abomination of architecture."

Today people still say about certain church edifices, "But it doesn't look like a church!" Usually this is said about structures built in the so-called modern or contemporary style. Somehow we identify churchliness with the building where we began our religious pilgrimage or with the type of structure that has become identified in our mind with the word "church." Yet human beings have managed to worship God in many different kinds of buildings and even in no structures at all.

Because it can broaden our outlook and form an interesting activity for the summer, adventuring in architecture is a worthwhile endeavor. In other words, we can take time to explore the church buildings in our community or in the area where we may be on vacation. This can be a project for an individual, a family or a group, perhaps a Sunday school class or a young people's organization.

Unfortunately or fortunately, we do not have ancient cathedrals to visit in this country. A trip through some of the great churches of Western Europe can be an enthralling experience. It is hard to imagine the painstaking work that went into one of these great buildings and even harder to grasp the spirit that moved people to erect such places for worship. At the same time it is sad to see what time has done to these old churches and to realize how much money is required to keep them from collapsing. But while we may lack great cathedrals, there is no lack of churches to visit in the United States and Canada.

Today most churches are kept locked when not in use because of the danger of thieves and vandals. This may seem a barrier for visiting but many churches have an office that is open, where you can obtain permission to view the building, and if you take time to phone ahead, most pastors or church secretaries are glad to open the church for you. People are usually proud of their church building and are anxious to show it off to visitors. If you plan to go with a group, it might be wise to schedule a number of visits on Saturday or Sunday afternoon. But do allow plenty of time at each building so you don't have to rush. You need time to look at the carving around the altar or study the symbols in the windows, for this is part of what makes adventuring in architecture enjoyable.

Before you begin such a project you need to learn a little about styles of churches. You could start by searching the New Testament to see what it says about church buildings and how they should be constructed. I will save you the time. The New Testament says nothing about this subject. *Nothing.* This seems strange, for architecture was very important in the world of the Old Testament. Exodus, Chapters 25, 26, and 27 contains detailed descriptions of the Tabernacle that Israel used for its worship for many years. 1 Kings, Chapters 6 and 7, tell how the Temple was constructed and where the furniture was placed. But the New Testament contains no parallel account for a Christian church. No one can say, with any biblical authority, "It doesn't look like a church!" When the biblical writers use the term "church" they mean a congregation, not a building.

However, Christians over the centuries have developed certain styles of architecture for worship and it helps to know something about this before starting on a pilgrimage of churches. The first believers apparently met in the homes of members and that process has been repeated many times. Paul in Romans 16:23 sends greetings from "my host Gaius, in whose house the church meets." Earlier in the same letter Paul greets Priscilla and Aquila and the church "that meets in their house."

When persecution arose, it became too dangerous to continue to meet in houses and so Christians worshiped in caves, in open air meetings and in the catacombs of Rome, the underground city where people were buried. The catacombs are still in existence and it gives you an eerie feeling to walk through these muddy passageways and remember that Christians once sang Jesus' praise under such conditions.

Christianity had a rags-to-riches transformation, however, when the Emperor Constantine granted this sect religious liberty and eventually made it the state religion. The number of worshipers increased so rapidly that it was no longer possible to hold services in homes. Church buildings now had to be erected and the style that seemed the most adaptable was the Roman law court, the basilica. This was a building, usually twice as long as it was wide, with massive pillars inside to hold up a flat roof. At one end there was a curved section, called an apse, where the bishop of the local congregation would sit, with the church elders on either side of him. The basilica was probably the first type of building that could be called a church.

Later this was followed by structures called "Romanesque." Here the roof was curved like half a barrel and the windows were rounded on top. The pillars were often eliminated but this meant that the walls had to be heavy and thick to support the massive roof. Also the windows had to be small so as not to weaken the walls. The design of the Romanesque church tends to be heavy and ponderous.

The next church style was the Gothic, which is still the type structure many feel is most "churchly." The Gothic church uses pointed arches, larger windows and buttresses or supports on the outside to hold up the walls and roof. The larger windows allow space for more stained glass work and the ornamentation inside and out is often very elaborate. John Milton was probably thinking of a Gothic church when he wrote:

> But let my due feet never fail,
> To walk the studious Cloysters pale.
> And love the high embowed Roof,
> With antick pillars massy proof,

And storied Windows richly dight,
Casting a dimm religious light.

*(Il Penseroso)*

The nineteenth century saw a great revival of interest in Gothic structures and many churches today embody some Gothic features.

Because it was popular when the early settlers came to America, the Georgian or Colonial style is still popular in this country. In this type of building the ornamentation is simple or nonexistent. Often there is a pillared porch outside the entranceway; inside, the walls may be white and the pews quite dark. Sometimes the pulpit rather than the altar dominates the building.

Rising costs and an interest in new types of building material have helped to produce the style known as "modern" or "contemporary." A great many modern buildings were erected after World War II. These are the structures that usually cause people to say, "But it doesn't look like a church," and some of these buildings seem ugly, but so do some of the older buildings. If you are interested in more architectural details, most libraries can furnish you with the books you need.

But the real enjoyment in visiting churches comes in seeing what people have built for worship, not in identifying styles. American churches are often a mixture of the past and the present. And no one says everyone must like the same thing. I once took a friend to visit a church building that had elaborate mosaics and paintings on the wall, and fancy, colored marble in the chancel. His verdict was that it was the biggest bunch of tomfoolery he had ever seen. Yet the people who worshiped there probably were very proud of their building. Different strokes for different folks.

We must not forget either that a church building always involves some compromises. The building site may dictate the shape of the structure, the architect may have to yield to certain influential members and always there is that important matter of money. I once visited a small Iowa town where the Lutheran church was the only contemporary building in the community. When I asked the custodian how they decided on such a design, he replied, "When we saw the plans, we didn't like them, but when we saw the price, we suddenly liked the drawings." From such mundane matters come great decisions. So don't go to criticize but to enjoy.

What should you look for on these expeditions? Obviously it is the interior of a church that is of prime importance, for this is where people sing their praises to God. The outside may impress the passerby, but only when we enter do we feel the lifeblood of the congregation. Some churches are foolers, with a rather unpromising exterior but with beautiful things inside. I know a church in Dubuque, Iowa, that has Tiffany glass windows that are a glory to behold but no one would guess the inner beauty from the rather drab exterior. So go in and sit down in a pew for awhile. Try to visualize the church filled with worshipers and with the sound of hymns rising to God. Katharine Morrison McClinton in her book, *The Changing Church* (pp. 15-17), says:

> The church is God's House and as such it must have a feeling of God. It must have beauty, spirituality and dignity. . . . A church should also express awe and wonder. It should stir the imagination. . . . A church should also

be Spartan in atmosphere, giving an appearance of strength and courage, for religion is never soft and easy.

Few buildings measure up to those standards, but we do need to get the feeling, the atmosphere of a building, when we visit it.

Next, approach the front, where the acts of worship center. This is called the chancel. Today most church buildings have an altar either against the wall or standing near the wall. In the days after the Reformation many churches demoted or abolished the altar and the pulpit took the center of attention, with the minister looking over the assembled congregation like an avenging angel as he preached. I once led the worship in a Scottish church where my eyes were on the level with the top of the balcony when I stood in the pulpit, and the congregation was far below me. If you find a church with a similar pattern, that will tell you something about the theology of that denomination as well as about their pattern of worship.

The chancel usually contains more than an altar, however. You may find there a communion rail, seats for the clergy, an organ, places for the choir, a baptismal font, the lectern where the lessons are read, and even the pulpit. Some chancels are wide and spacious, others deep and crowded. It is wise to ask permission before entering the chancel area, for some denominations reserve the chancel rigidly for the clergy and insist that lay members stay in the nave or auditorium.

The windows of a church also deserve careful study. Some windows are just spaces that let in light and air. But most churches use the windows to help beautify the building. In medieval times, when few could read, the church windows became illustrated sermons telling the congregation Bible stories, and this practice has continued down to the present. So some church windows are simple glass panels, some are pictures in glass, and some contain abstract patterns or symbols of the church. In recent years there has been a revival of interest in stained glass and you may want to learn more about it. Windows are a fascinating part of adventuring in architecture.

Sometimes you will find odd touches and unique features in a building. I once saw a baptismal font that had been made out of wrought iron by the local blacksmith. It resembled a gigantic potted Easter lily and one of the blossoms could be removed and replaced by an iron bowl when there was a baptism. The minister indicated that this was a rare specimen and by his tone made plain that he wished it were so rare as to be nonexistent. Yet I have no doubt that an earnest Christian labored many hours to make this strange font. Perhaps the Good Lord appreciated it, even if the minister didn't.

As you visit, look for signs of love and concern in the church furnishings. Engraved inscriptions speak of love and sorrow for someone who has gone. You may see hand-embroidered kneeling cushions and beautifully made pulpit hangings. Or you may find signs of soil and neglect that speak of a congregation where nobody cares. I preached in a building some time ago where the robes worn by the acolytes looked as if they had been slept in for a week. So it goes.

You may want to take some notes as you visit various churches. That will help you remember what you have seen. You may even get some ideas to take back to your own church group, for no one has all the good ideas in church building and we can borrow from one another. But above all, adventuring in architecture will give you an idea of the various types of structure which people have built to worship God. It will help you see how deeply ingrained in us is the longing to come into the presence of God. You will be impressed by the variety of human religious feelings. Adventuring in architecture may even keep you from ever saying again, "It doesn't look like a church!"

# Roots

When did the church you belong to hold its first service? Who were the charter members? Why did the congregation choose the building site where you now worship? How many young men or women from this fellowship have entered full-time Christian service? Unless you are a very unusual individual, you probably don't know the answer to any of these questions. They deal with past history and most of us aren't interested in the past.

Yet history can be a fascinating study, particularly when it is concerned about things close at home. The events of bygone days cast interesting shadows on the present. And Americans are beginning to explore some of the side trails and forgotten nooks of the past. Perhaps Alex Haley with his best seller *Roots* is responsible for some of our nostalgia. The Bicentennial celebration also made many Americans more conscious of the world of their ancestors. People today are busily exploring their family tree, sometimes a little fearful of what they will find there, but determined to learn something about their past history.

Your church also has a past. Every congregation has its own roots. The sign on the door of the archives of The American Lutheran Church says "Roots Cellar." Behind the door in Dubuque, Iowa, are the records of hundreds of congregations with booklets, pictures, and other documents telling of past history. Most Christian denominations maintain similar "roots cellars." But only the individual members of a congregation are in a position to learn about the real roots, the daily experiences in the past that have contributed to the present existence of the local church.

Here is an interesting opportunity to do something different in the summer, to engage in an activity that will benefit you and the entire congregation. Why not begin a "roots" search for some of the historical sidelights of your local church? You can conduct this search by yourself, enlist the aid of members of your family or work with a committee of similar-minded church members. In the course of such a search you may uncover some inspiring and fascinating stories of Christian sacrifice and devotion. Some of our ancestors had to pay dearly to keep the church alive. You may also stumble on some dark pages about quarreling and denominational fights that you may think better forgotten, but this is all a part of the fascination of uncovering the past. When you turn over a stone you may find a diamond or a bug underneath.

How do you start? First it is wise to get approval for your project from the pastor and the church vestry. This will make people understand that you are not just a nosy parker when you question them about their actions and memories but are engaged in important work. It will help to have a brief notice put in the church bulletin to alert members of the congregation to your project and to seek their help with documents and reminiscences. Attics and closets may yield much that is valuable.

Next, see what records are already available. Official church records are useful but they aren't always accurate, for some pastors are meticulous, some very careless, and church secretaries are a modern innovation. You may also find some material already gathered and published in an anniversary booklet or stuffed away in a file somewhere. Copies of church bulletins may be useful, although few people keep these weekly publications. I once knew a man who kept several copies of every bulletin published by a new church. When his wife insisted that this was silly, he told her: "The time will come when you won't be able to find these bulletins anyplace." That was true and you may uncover a cache of old bulletins to aid your project.

One of the rich sources of "roots" material is a collection of old photographs. What we wouldn't give to have a photographic record of that first church formed in Jerusalem on Pentecost. We will have to be content with material from this century and a part of the last. There is something fascinating about old faded pictures showing confirmation classes or Sunday school picnics, with all the people dressed in odd costumes. Such glimpses of the past should make us reflect on what people, fifty years from now, will think of our present-day clothing and hairstyles. One of the great problems with photographs is that photographers seldom recorded the names of the people on the pictures. Recently while attending a congregational anniversary celebration I noted with amusement the frantic attempts and the disagreements as people tried to identify former members of the congregation. Some of the older church members can be of help in identifying the past, although distance often lends confusion as well as enchantment.

Very early in your search you will want to draw up a chronology of events, listing outstanding events and the periods when various pastors served at this location. But history is not just names and dates. The really important things in a study of roots are the stories and anecdotes that have lingered in people's minds. It will help to gather some of the older members together and let them search the past for what happened to them or their parents and grandparents. A tape recorder, placed unobtrusively in the midst, will guarantee the accuracy of what is said, although reminiscences have a way of changing and growing over the years. But there will be many treasured stories.

I know a congregation that will never forget how the new preacher got so excited the first Sunday he preached that he pounded the pulpit and broke the bookstand in two. One of the members kept the broken wood and presented it to the minister when he left to assume another position. I know a congregation that received an unforgettable shock one Sunday morning when a guest speaker had to announce that the pastor had been killed on vacation. A friend of mine has a written account of how his father, a pioneer Lutheran preacher, was almost killed in a prairie fire when returning from giving communion to a dying member. You may not discover anything so amusing, so tragic or dramatic as the above stories but every congregation has its interesting moments.

A search for congregational roots can be an interesting study for the summer but it should not stop there. All information gathered should be kept and augmented with both new and old material when available. Church archivists will often microfilm important congregational documents so that there will be a permanent record, stored in a safe place. Fire, insects, and neglect have destroyed much valuable material in the past. Perhaps you or someone else in the congregation can take charge of keeping the local archives. You may even find that you have gathered enough interesting material to warrant its publication in a small booklet.

Carl Sandburg once wrote: "I tell you, the past is a bucket of ashes." I don't believe he really meant that, for he wrote a long multivolumed history of the life of Abraham Lincoln. The past *can* be dull as ashes and as useless but it can also be a living witness as it shows us God's hand in the history of a Christian congregation.

# Your Neighbor's Faith

Drop a glass plate from the top of a ten-story building onto the concrete sidewalk below. The result is certain. The plate will be shattered into dozens or perhaps hundreds of pieces. That fragmented plate is a good symbol of the shattered unity of the Christian church except that the church didn't come apart all at once. Although Jesus prayed that his followers would remain united, Christians have not fulfilled his prayer. They have quarreled and divided the church into hundreds of different groups. The church is like a shattered glass plate.

No one knows exactly how many denominations there are, for churches keep splitting, reuniting, and disappearing. The latest edition of *Handbook of Denominations in the United States* lists more than 250 organizations on this continent alone. The churches described in this book include such exotics as Church of God (Abrahamic Faith), Two Seed in the Spirit Predestinarian Baptists, Church of Christ (Temple Lot), Kodesh Church of Immanuel, National David Spiritual Temple of Christ Church Union (Inc.) U.S.A., and Triumph the Church and Kingdom of

God in Christ, as well as familiar denominations like the Roman Catholics, Lutherans, and Presbyterians.

Much as we may regret that the unity which the church had on Pentecost has been shattered, we will have to live with a divided Christendom. In recent years the ecumenical movement has promoted better feeling among Christians but the divisions still remain. The church seems like the ill-fated Humpty Dumpty—all the king's horses and all the king's men can't put it back together again.

Although we may not be able to heal the breaches in Christendom, there is something we can do and it forms an ideal activity for the summer season. We can learn something about other Christian churches. For unfortunately most of us have strange and erroneous ideas about our neighbor's faith and we haven't taken time to check out the facts. Josh Billings once said that it wasn't ignorance that caused most of the trouble in this world, it was that people "knew so danged much that ain't so." That's probably particularly true in the area of religion. Unless we have made a special study of the subject, we are probably still repeating the old cliches about others. People still accuse the Episcopalians of being rich and snooty, insist the Lutherans are just like the Roman Catholics, Methodists are all bluenoses, etc. The early church had to endure this kind of slander from its pagan neighbors, who insisted that Christians were atheists and cannibals. In fact, Jesus warned his disciples that enemies would say all kinds of evil against them falsely, but there is no justification for Christians to slander their fellow believers.

So, why not use some of your time in the summer to do some exploring and to learn about your neighbor's faith? Whether you are away from home in a place where there may be no church of your denomination or simply taking a Sunday off from your own church, the summer offers you a good time to visit a different group and learn something about their faith and worship.

If possible, it will help to do a little reading and boning up before making your visit. The *Handbook,* mentioned earlier, offers a simple, unbiased summary of various denominations, but you may find other books and pamphlets that will help. We are all the products of our history and we never escape completely from the past, so a little church history may be helpful. Thus the Lutheran church arose out of a doctrinal struggle and Lutherans are still vitally interested in correct doctrine. Methodism came into being as a movement to revive the spiritual life of the Church of England, and Methodists still stress Christian living. So it goes. Of course you should not overstress the background, for times change and there has often been a rethinking of a doctrinal point or a change in practice through the years.

Reading about the worship of another group can also help you avoid embarrassing mistakes. I know a Scottish woman who was familiar with the custom in her church of placing the offering into a receptacle in the vestibule before entering the church proper. She visited a Roman Catholic church one Sunday and observed everyone stopping to dip their fingers into the holy water but she misunderstood and deposited her money into the bowl before she realized her mistake. The result was confusion and embarrassment, with the money having to be fished out and fresh water blessed and placed in the container. The woman laughed as she told her story later, but for the moment it was a traumatic experience. So a little study may help, although you can usually get by if you watch the actions of others.

Well, suppose you have decided to visit a certain church and have read what you could about the group. What next? If you have a friend who belongs to that denomination, it might be wise to ask if you can accompany him or her to the church. But if you must go alone or with the members of your family, first check on the time of services. Churches are notoriously lax about letting everyone know when they change to a summer schedule, and bulletin boards don't always mean what they say. It is embarrassing to come into the church after the services have begun and you may be even more chagrinned to arrive and find the congregation filing out—the worship is conducted an hour earlier during the summer months. So check. Then plan to arrive at the church a little ahead of time, but not too early. You want to be in a position to observe what others do.

You should leave no doubt in anyone's mind that you are a visitor, not a spy, and not a prospective member. Many churches consider a stranger an immediate candidate for conversion, and you may find yourself on a prospect list if you don't make clear that you are a visitor, nothing more. Often churches have literature available in the vestibule and it may be helpful to take some of this material, for it will tell you about the church's doctrine and emphasis.

First impressions are always important, but don't judge an entire denomination by what happens on one visit. Some churches specialize in glad handing and making the visitor feel at home. You may get the royal treatment. Other churches emphasize the solemnity of worship and may leave you strictly on your own. Neither approach is necessarily an indication of the spiritual life of a congregation or an entire religious group.

The form of worship will be different from the one you are familiar with, but most churches these days provide worshipers with a bulletin which indicates the order of the service. A friendly church member may also assist you. But church hymnals can be traps for the unwary as they are printed for use by members and you may get lost at times. What is important is that you note the similarities and differences to your own church worship. Most Protestant services have a common background and churches are moving closer to a common form of service, but customs vary. I remember a member who was very upset when he attended a denomination where they sang the doxology at the opening of worship. He couldn't understand why they would so such a thing, but it is as logical to praise God at the beginning of church worship as at the end.

There is a familiar story about a man who visited a friend's church and at every point in the service demanded to know: "What does that mean?" When the minister got in the pulpit and looked at his watch before beginning the sermon, the visitor again asked: "What does that mean?" The friend, disgusted at long-winded sermons, replied, "That doesn't mean a thing." Not everything done in a church service has some symbolic meaning but you need to be alert to the customs of the group.

After services, visit with the members and the pastor. Someone will be glad to show you around the church and answer any questions you may have. It will help when you get home to jot down your impressions. Later you should check these with someone who knows about that church.

Of course, one visit to a church will not tell you all about a group and neither will a quick reading of a book on the subject. There are overtones and hidden ties to a denomination and these cannot always be put into words. Some denominations have strong economic and nationalistic ties and these things also affect the worship and the mystique of the faith. But at least you will have some impression of another denomination. You may find that your opinion of another church has been in error.

Some have feared that if we visit other people's churches, we may be led away from our own faith. But this is extremely unlikely to occur. A number of years ago many Sunday school classes in The American Lutheran Church conducted visits to neighboring churches. The result of such visits was that while the groups learned much about other churches, the young people all felt more contented with their own form of worship. The grass isn't always greener on the other side of the fence and it doesn't do any harm to observe our neighbor's grass. A visit to a church of another denomination can be a useful and stimulating thing for a Christian to do in the summer.

# Rally Day

Sunday schools once celebrated a special occasion each year called Rally Day. Perhaps many continue this custom. Rally Day was the time when everyone was expected back from vacation and when the normal program of the church was resumed. About a week before the designated day, each Sunday school pupil received a card in the mail, urging him or her to be present on the following Sunday. When you arrived you received a button or a badge, indicating that you were present on Rally Day. Generally there was special music, a word of greeting from the minister himself, and at times a special treat of candy for those who "rallied." Also pupils were promoted at this time and often there was anxiety over whether the new teacher might not be as good or as lenient as the former one.

There is something nice about the concept of Rally Day. It says to everyone that the summer is over, the visiting and the vacations are finished. It is time to resume the full-scale program of the church. Actually, for most congregations, the fall season is the time when the church year begins, even though custom makes the fourth Sunday before Christmas the start of the official church year. So the Pentecost season has a sharp break in it; it is divided into the summer vacation time and the fall season of activity. Of course, congregations continue to operate during the months of June, July, and August, but most groups do have a period of modified activity during the summer.

This is as it should be. To paraphrase Ecclesiastes, "There is a time to travel and visit, and a time to get back to work, a time to explore God's world out-of-doors, and a time to resume the program of church activity."

Only, you cannot divide life into watertight compartments. One of the things that parents notice when school begins again is that their children haven't taken a vacation from growing. Clothes no longer fit and last year's pair of shoes pinches horribly. Growth takes no holiday when you are young. What is true of the physical nature of human beings should also be true of our spiritual life. Summer should be a time of growth for all of us. Did you ever notice how often Jesus uses the symbol of growth to describe life in his kingdom? The sower sows seed and it produces a harvest. The kingdom of heaven is like a mustard seed, so small at first yet finally becoming a large bush where birds can find food and shelter. The fig tree which produces no fruit is cursed and dies. All these symbols stress the importance of change, of growth for the Christian.

The summer section of the Pentecost season should be a time of growth for the believer. Rally Day should find us closer to God than when the hot mcnths of summer began. For we are not to take a vacation from God and then return to him in the fall. Either through some of the activities suggested in the preceding chapters or through some plans of our own, we should grow in knowledge and appreciation of God during the summer months. The fall season should be a time of getting back into the groove again, but another name for groove is "rut," and we should not settle into a rut. We should be a different and better person because we have allowed God to fill our hearts with his grace during the summer. In the words of an old hymn, we should be able to sing: "More love to thee, O Christ, More love to thee."

PART III | **Devotions for Pentecost**

The following thirty brief devotions are all based on passages from the New Testament that speak about the Holy Spirit and us. The passages chosen are concentrated in certain books because some New Testament writers have more to say about the Holy Spirit than others. The devotions are not intended to present a complete doctrinal view of the Spirit nor are they directed at answering some of the problems recently raised in the church about the gifts of the Spirit. Rather it is hoped that by looking at the wide range of material about the Spirit and his work, the reader will gain a greater appreciation of the Third Person of the Trinity and his involvement in our lives.

# IN AT THE BEGINNING

The creation of the world. The coming of the Son of God in human flesh. Those are the two most important events in human history. *And the Spirit of God was present on both occasions.* In the Genesis account, the Spirit moved on the face of the waters. In the annunciation, Mary is told that the Holy Spirit will overshadow her. How simply and delicately the writers tell the story. But the Holy Spirit was present at the beginning of both events.

We may be tempted to say, "How wonderful, but it doesn't concern me." And in a sense that is true. The world was made and Christ was born without either our involvement or our permission. Yet the pattern that God followed is one that should commend itself to us. If those two great events needed the presence of the Spirit, isn't it logical to desire his presence in the events of our life too?

When we begin a new job, we need the Spirit. When we get married, when we take a trip, when we join a group in some activity, when we take on the responsibility of parenthood, we should ask for the help that the Holy Spirit can give us. In the words of a hymn celebrating the Trinity:

> Come, Holy Comforter,
> Thy sacred witness bear
> In this glad hour:

And the Spirit should be there at the beginning. Too often people wait until they get into trouble.

Then they think about God and call to him for help. Of course it's better late than never, but it is also better early than late.

Actually, every day is a new beginning. The world begins again for us every twenty-four hours. The Son of God is born again in our hearts. And so we need the Spirit to guide us, to comfort us, to give us strength. If he's in at the beginning, the day will go well.

*Holy Spirit, be with me today. Fill my heart with love and my mind with truth. In Jesus' name, Amen.*

**Matthew 28:16-20**

# ONLY ONE GOD

"In the name of the Father and of the Son and of the Holy Spirit." This is almost the first time the Trinity is mentioned in the Bible. The stress in the Old Testament is on the oneness of God. "Hear, O Israel, the Lord our God, the Lord is one." That was God's message to Israel.

In the New Testament we begin to get some idea of the complex nature of the one whom we call God. We learn to know him as Father, as Son, as Holy Spirit. The Christian church has spent many weary centuries arguing about how God can be triune in his nature. There is no reason to prolong that argument.

But perhaps we need to stress again the unity of God. As we meditate on the relationship between the Holy Spirit and us, we must remember that we are not dealing with one-third of God. The Spirit is not different from the Son or the Father. He simply deals with us in a different area of life.

100

It is particularly meaningful that all three persons are mentioned in connection with our baptism, for baptism is closely connected with our salvation. Father, Son, and Holy Spirit are all concerned with our being saved. Sometimes God the Father is pictured as being opposed to human beings and only being won over by the pleadings of the Son. And God the Holy Spirit is made an afterthought, a Johnny-come-lately who appears on the scene after Jesus has done all the work. That's a shocking distortion of the biblical picture.

It is God who works to save us, God, Father, Son, and Holy Spirit. It is good to think about the specific work of the Spirit, but we dare never forget that there is only one *God*.

One of the great hymns of the church is "Come, Thou Almighty King." The author devotes a verse to each member of the Trinity but then adds:

> To thee, great One in Three,
> Eternal praises be
>    Hence evermore!
> Thy sovereign majesty
> May we in glory see,
> And to eternity
>    Love and adore.
>        (*LBW*, 522)

*Lord, Triune God, we do adore you. Amen.*

Luke 11:9-13

# HOW CAN I BE SURE?

How can I know? How can I be sure that I have the Holy Spirit and that I am a true Christian? The search for certainty is an old one in the church.

Thomas wanted proof of Jesus' resurrection. Luther sought to be reassured that his sins were forgiven. Many people today look for some special signs of the presence of the Spirit so that they can be sure they are saved. How can you be sure?

Of course the answer is—You can't. No certificate is going to float down from heaven saying you are a genuine certified Christian and have the Holy Spirit. No special signs are promised to us. For Christianity is based on a single word—faith. And faith means trust, it means walking confidently even when you aren't sure. It is the evidence of things not seen. There are no irrefutable proofs that we have the Holy Spirit.

But notice what Jesus says on this subject. He promises that God will give the Holy Spirit to all who ask. Jesus points out that a human father would not disappoint or mistreat his children by giving them something evil when they ask for the good. Then comes the comparison—How much more will God be willing to give us the Spirit if we ask for it?

And that's as far as we can go. God has promised us his Spirit. What kind of Christians would we be to say, "Maybe you're lying, God. Give me some proof." No one would actually say that, but if we fret about whether we are saved or whether we have the Holy Spirit, we are implying that God is untruthful. And that's very foolish.

Sometimes we say about an honest man, "His word is as good as his bond." By that we mean that we can trust him despite everything. Well, God is like that. We can rely on him. If he promises us the Holy Spirit then we shall have the Holy Spirit. All we need to do is ask.

Come, gracious Spirit, heavenly dove,
With light and comfort from above.
Come be our guardian and our guide,
O'er every thought and step preside.

(*LBW*, 475)

*Lord, give me a full measure of your Spirit. May I
not doubt but walk by faith. Amen.*

John 3:5-8

# YOU NEVER CAN TELL

The following inscription appears on a tombstone
in an English church:

> John Newton, clerk, once an Infidel and liber-
> tine, a servant of slavers in Africa, was, by the
> rich Mercy of our Lord and Saviour Jesus
> Christ, Preserved, restored, pardoned, and ap-
> pointed to preach the Faith he had long la-
> boured to destroy.

Those words sum up the life of John Newton who
changed from a dealer in human bodies to a preacher
to human souls. Newton wrote a beautiful hymn to
mark his change of life.

Amazing grace, how sweet the sound,
That saved a wretch like me!
I once was lost, but now am found;
Was blind, but now I see.

(*LBW*, 448)

No one would have chosen John Newton as a good
prospect for church membership, much less as a candidate for the Christian ministry. Yet the Holy Spirit

103

touched his heart and Newton became a blessing to many people. You never can tell!

All life is unpredictable. A stormy day may end with a beautiful sunset. An ugly duckling may become a beautiful swan. A stupid schoolboy may turn out to be Winston Churchill. You never can tell.

And the Holy Spirit also possesses this unpredictability, at least as far as we are concerned. Jesus uses the coming and going of the wind to describe to Nicodemus how people are born of the Spirit. There are no signs to tell you who will listen and who will reject the gospel. There is no formula that says that ten sermons or ten Bible verses or five acts of love will open the door of the human heart. We must simply do our best to share the gospel with everyone we come in contact with. We dare not classify anyone as an unlikely prospect. For the Spirit moves in his own mysterious way. He comes and goes as he pleases. You never can tell.

*Lord, help me to be a faithful witness to others. Bless the words I speak and the things I do so that those I meet may see Christ in me and learn to love him. Amen.*

John 7:37-39

# HIDDEN RESOURCES

When an army tried to capture an ancient walled city it sometimes attempted to batter down the walls. More often though the besiegers tried to starve out the inhabitants and this was an easy task if the city's drinking water was located outside the walls. In a short time the inhabitants would be perishing of thirst and the battle would be won.

But many cities had a supply of water inside the city limits. Jerusalem was such a city and this hidden resource made it almost invulnerable to attack. The water kept the people alive and fighting against their enemies.

Modern warfare has changed all that, but the principle of hidden resources is still a practical one. And Jesus indicates that the Holy Spirit is such a resource for the Christian. He is like a river of water flowing out of the heart. The claim by Jesus comes close to his words to the woman at the well:

> Whoever drinks of the water that I shall give him will never thirst; the water that I shall give him will become a spring of water in him welling up to eternal life.

The Spirit is a resource, giving us life and strength whenever we need help.

Did you ever observe a Christian who seemed to have the necessary endurance to win through all kinds of adversities? That was the hidden resource, the Holy Spirit in action. Did you ever have to face a challenge that seemed too strong for you and yet suddenly you found strength that you didn't know you had? That's the Holy Spirit, pouring out the streams of living water.

Moreover, this hidden resource can be of help to others. When the Spirit sustains us, our example can give others courage to go ahead. One Christian whose heart is overflowing with God's Spirit can inspire a whole household or an entire church. One is reminded of the Christmas song, "God King Wenceslas," where the page follows in the king's footsteps and we are told

Heat was in the very sod
Which the Saint had printed. (Walked)

*Lord, let the streams of living water flow in my heart. Give me strength each day for the challenges that I must face. Amen.*

**John 14:25-26**

# THE GREAT EDUCATOR

There are two popular ideas about education today. Some people believe that you go to school, graduate, and then you are educated. The job is completed; there is no need for further study. Others think of education as an ongoing process that never ends as long as we are alive.

Unfortunately, many Christians believe in the first theory. They attend Sunday school when they are young and perhaps attend some confirmation classes and then, on being received into church membership, they have graduated. They don't need to learn any more.

The Holy Spirit doesn't espouse that idea at all. Jesus pictures the Spirit as one who will guide the believers into all that Jesus had told them. In other words, the Holy Spirit is a teacher and we can never exhaust the areas of truth if we let him lead us.

At the heart of Christianity, of course, there is a very simple message. The early church summed it up with the confession, "Jesus is Lord." John 3:16 is often called the gospel in miniature. The whole truth is found there. Yet the Bible is a textbook with many further teachings and the Spirit is eager to lead us into additional areas of truth. As an old song puts it:

106

Thy Word is like a deep, deep mine,
And jewels rich and rare
Are hidden in its mighty depths
For every searcher there.

But since knowledge doesn't save us, why should we seek further education? If we know that we are saved by the grace of God, isn't that enough? If that were so, why should God have given us the rest of the Bible? Actually the teachings of the Bible can help us meet the challenges of daily life. The Spirit can guide us through temptation and doubt. Others may need help to find Christ, but if we don't know what Jesus said and did, we cannot help them. No Christian ever knows too much of God's truth. We don't graduate from the school run by the Holy Spirit. There is always another jewel to be found, another truth that the Spirit wants to share with us.

*Lord, give me a hunger for your truth. May the Spirit guide me each day into new paths of learning. Amen.*

**John 16:1-7**

# TROUBLE, TROUBLE EVERYWHERE

Martin Luther, in a sermon delivered at Pentecost used the following words to describe the situation which the disciples faced when Jesus left them:

All the world will be against you; and the devil will be at your heels, and with his venomous, blasphemous tongue will say the worst about you and will accuse you and decry you before all the world as cheats and rebels. Besides, your own conscience and heart will plague and frighten you with the fear of God's wrath, with sadness and heavy thoughts of your own weakness, so that you well may and must despair if you were to be left without comfort and strength in this predicament.

Those are strong words, and if Luther had stopped there the picture would have been hopeless. But he went on to talk about the Comforter, the Counselor whom Jesus promised his followers. The Holy Spirit was Jesus' answer to the anxiety of the disciples, faced with living in a world without their Lord.

Of course, you and I live in a different world than those first Christians and yet the situation isn't as different as we might imagine. We still face trouble without and within. No one is trying to persecute us and yet the casual scorn that many have for religion today does affect us. The luxuries of our present society do tempt us to look away from God. And our consciences still prick us. Sin may be an old-fashioned word, yet guilt is still found in human hearts today.

We need the Comforter too, and what a joy it is to know that the Holy Spirit comes to us in our need. That doesn't mean that the purpose of our Christianity is to make us feel good. Some people use religion as a kind of tranquilizer. But it is reassuring to know that we are not alone in this world. The Spirit speaks to us through the Word of God, through worship, and through fellow Christians. There may be trouble everywhere but we have One who helps us face those troubles.

*Lord, I do not ask to live in a trouble-free world. But I ask that the Spirit be with me every day. Forgive me when I fail and strengthen me when I grow weak. Amen.*

**John 16:8-11**

# THE GREAT VICTORY

"Behold, this child is set for the fall and rising of many in Israel, and a sign that is spoken against" (Luke 2:34). The words were spoken by Simeon when he saw the infant Jesus in the temple. They remind us that Jesus Christ represents a turning point in human history, a cleavage between the children of God and the people of darkness. And the work of proclaiming that separation is performed by the Holy Spirit. Note the three steps of fulfillment of Simeon's prophecy.

*He will convince the world of sin.* Sin is a broad word but the sin which Jesus is talking about is the sin of rejecting him. The Holy Spirit began that work on Pentecost when the people, moved by Peter's sermon, said, "Brethren, what shall we do?" The Spirit continues to witness to the sin of rejecting God's gracious offer in Christ.

*Of righteousness.* Jesus was crucified as a sinner, a lawbreaker, a false teacher. Yet Jesus was vindicated in the Resurrection. He was the righteous one, his enemies were the sinners. It is the business of the Spirit to defend Jesus against those who attack him, since Jesus is no longer here in person. Through the Word of God we are called to believe in the righteous Son of God.

*Of judgment.* How quickly the tables were turned

on Easter. On Good Friday evil men judged Jesus and the rulers of this world seemed victorious. The accusing voice of Jesus had been silenced, apparently forever. Yet it was not Jesus who was judged but his enemies. God won the victory on Easter and it was total, complete.

It is this victory which the Spirit tells us about in the New Testament. It has been won for us. The prophecy of Simeon came true. And we are called on to rejoice and to take part in the victory celebration. The Christian message is good news, tidings of great joy because it tells of God's victory.

*Lord, may we never grow tired of hearing about your victory. Reassure us again and again that we have been blessed by Christ's conquering of sin and death. In his name, Amen.*

**John 16:12-15**

## THE SPIRIT OF TRUTH

The cynical Pontius Pilate asked, "What is truth?" Then he didn't wait for an answer because he didn't believe there was an answer. Most of us share a little of that cynicism. We have been told too many times, "This is the truth," only to find that the newspaper the next day denies the whole story. Yet there is one place where we can be sure, for Jesus calls the Holy Spirit, "the Spirit of truth."

Just what does that mean? Some think that the Holy Spirit will answer all their problems, that he will tell them what kind of necktie to wear, the type of job they should choose, even the person they should marry. Of course we cannot put limitations on God, but Jesus is really saying that the Spirit will be his spokesman in the world. "He will glorify me, for he will take what is mine and declare it to you." This is the basic work of the Spirit, to be a witness for Jesus Christ.

It is easy to see why we need this Spirit. When Jesus was here, his disciples could take their questions to him and receive an answer. Teach us how to pray. Who is greatest in the kingdom? What are the signs of your return? These are some of the requests they presented to Jesus.

Now another voice is needed. We need the Spirit of Truth to guide us as we face new problems and new challenges. We need to know what Jesus would have us do. And the Spirit is called on to lead us.

That doesn't mean that the Spirit will do what we can do for ourselves. He will not explain the Einstein theory or describe how the law of gravity works or even tell us what kind of building materials to use in a church building.

But he will speak where Jesus would speak. He will tell us about the hope which we have that our Lord will return. He will guide the church in matters that affect salvation. We dare not be cynical here. We must listen to the Spirit of Truth.

*Lord, speak to me through your spirit so that I may understand, and then move me to follow the truth. Amen.*

# GOD'S DYNAMITE

The Spirit animates God's Word and makes it live. He really does. He calls people all the time. He grabs them up into his life and mission. He turns them on to newness of life in his name. It surprises me to realize how potent and dynamic the Spirit's work, in the ongoing life of the church really is.

This quotation appears on page 154 of an excellent book about the Holy Spirit, called *Touched by the Spirit,* written by Dr. Richard A. Jensen. Perhaps this picture of a powerful Spirit seems farfetched. Yet look at what happened when the Spirit came on Pentecost. Before that time, the disciples had fled like rabbits when Jesus was arrested. Even after the resurrection when he told them he was going away they still wanted to know if he was ready to restore the kingdom to Israel. They wanted Jesus to do the work.

But look at the disciples after Pentecost. Now they are bold as lions, preaching openly, defying the authorities, risking their lives for the sake of the gospel. They had received power from the Spirit, they had God's dynamite in their hearts. This Spirit is no fluttering dove. He is power, POWER, POWER.

But we live in a tamer, more blasé world. Can God's Spirit still move people? Or has his get up and go, gotten up and gone? The answer is all around you. Think of the Christians who defied Hitler. The Spirit gave them power. Think of Christians in communist countries who live under constant pressure from the civil authorities and yet who remain faithful to their Lord.

Or look into the hearts and lives of thousands of ordinary people who face great difficulties in life and yet who find help through the Word of God and prayer. The Spirit still has power to move human beings.

John Bunyan in *Pilgrim's Progress* describes how Christian sees a fire that keeps burning even though the devil pours water on it. Then the pilgrim is shown the Holy Spirit pouring oil on the fire of the human heart and that keeps the fire alive. The Spirit of God still does that. He is God's power to keep alive the fire in our hearts.

*Holy Spirit, give me power. May I be alive with the fire of the gospel and eager to share your love with everyone I meet. In Jesus' name. Amen.*

**Acts 2:17-21**

# LIVING AT THE END

A Christian who longed for the return of Christ got into the habit of looking at the sky each morning and saying, "Maybe today, Lord?" We may marvel at his faith or wonder at his presumption, but every human being is living the last days. The words from Joel that Peter quoted at Pentecost proclaim that fact.

"Living in the last days." This sounds confusing. How could people in the first century talk about living at the end when here it is, 1900 years later and Christ hasn't yet returned? Did Peter misuse Joel's words in the excitement of Pentecost? Did people in Peter's day say, "Maybe today, Lord?"

Some Christians have solved this problem with a

113

statement from 2 Peter where the author says that a day in God's sight is like a thousand years and a thousand years as a day. So they figure we are only into the second day in God's time. But there is something deeper to be learned from the expression, "the last days." Look at the picture of God's time as recorded in the Bible. For a long period God worked with the children of Israel, and made of them "a royal priesthood, a holy nation." Also, for a brief period of time—about thirty-three years—God worked through Jesus Christ. In addition, God works through the Holy Spirit. Only Christ's return and the judgment of all mankind remain. So, regardless of how long the earth continues, these are the last days.

It shouldn't frighten us to be told that we live in the last days. It means that we have the full revelation of God's work of salvation. We have the Bible. We can see and learn about the work of God, Father, Son, and Holy Spirit. These are the last days as we await the return of Christ. Maybe today, Lord? Maybe we will live to see our Lord's return.

*Thank you, Lord, for your gift of salvation. May I always be ready for your return. Amen.*

**Acts 5:1-11**

# YOU CAN'T FOOL GOD

The story of Ananias and Sapphira is a shocking one. The sad ending brought great fear into the hearts of those first Christians. Many, reading the story today, feel that the punishment was greater than the crime, but we can't sit down at this late date and pass judgment on the events. All we know is that the wily couple tried to pull a fast one on the early church and were caught in the act. Their consciences probably caused the sad ending.

There is a simple point to all this—you can't lie to God. We don't know how Peter learned about the sinful action of the guilty pair but we know how the Holy Spirit learned the truth. *God sees in the heart.* God's Spirit knows us better than we know ourselves. As the author of Psalm 139 tells us:

> O Lord, thou hast searched me and known me!
> Thou knowest when I sit down and when I rise up;
>   thou discernest my thoughts from afar.

Later on the writer adds:

> Even the darkness is not dark to thee,
>   the night is bright as the day;
>   for darkness is as light with thee.

It seems foolish to try to play games with God. Yet people do it. They make promises to God and don't keep them. They deny their sins. They think God can be bribed by certain good actions.

The story of Ananias and Sapphira provides the answer to all this. There is no way to fool God, no way we can deceive the Holy Spirit. He knows what goes on in the deepest darkness. Our life is an open book to him.

A young boy came out of the principal's office, saying, "I can't lie to him. He sees right through you." The Spirit of God does just that. He knows. That doesn't make God our enemy. It simply means that we can't fool him. We must deal with God in fairness and honesty.

The story of the Pharisee and the Publican is a case in point. The publican was honest with God. And he was the one who received the blessing. You can't fool God.

*Lord, you know my weaknesses and my needs. Forgive me and help me to deal honestly with you and with all people. Amen.*

Acts 6:1-3; 7:54-56

# A PART-TIME JOB?

Wanted: part-time Christians. Must be willing to devote some time to God and to have some faith in the Bible. No great sacrifice required. If interested, contact Zion Church.

You never saw an ad like that and you never will. For Christianity asks total commitment, not partial allegiance. As the character from *Oklahoma* puts it: "Is it all or nothin' with you?"

Notice the strange language in the two readings for today—"seven men of good repute, *full* of the Spirit," "but he, *full* of the Holy Spirit." That's a favorite expression with Luke. The disciples were *filled* with the Spirit when they spoke on Pentecost. Peter was *filled* with the Spirit when he spoke before the Jewish court. Paul was *filled* with the Holy Spirit when he denounced the magician, Elymas.

What does it mean to be filled with the Spirit? Is this a kind of ecstasy, a religious spell, a fanatical zeal? Not at all. It simply means that the individual has yielded totally to Christ, totally to God's spirit. All other considerations have been laid aside. The

116

seven deacons would not play favorites among the needy widows. Stephen did not think about his own safety. The desire to serve God filled the whole person. There wasn't room for any other thoughts or ideas.

How important it is to be *filled* with the Spirit, for most of us have good intentions, good goals in life. The difficulty is that other considerations check our good impulses. We have the Spirit, but only on a part-time basis. He has to share our heart with so many other things. And that ends in disaster.

The human heart is only so big. There is only room for the Spirit. We must learn to sing:

Have Thine own way, Lord, Have Thine own way!
Hold o'er my being Absolute sway!
Fill with Thy Spirit Till all shall see
Christ only, always, living in me!

*Lord, fill me with your Spirit so that my joy and desire is to love and serve you. Amen.*

**Acts 7:51-56**

# DON'T BE STUPID

There is no sadder story in the Bible than the rejection of God by many of his people. Israel had for centuries tried to change the allegiance of their neighbors from false gods to the God of Abraham, Isaac, and Jacob—but with little success. When God visited this earth in the person of Jesus, the story was the same—rejection. And rejection, in the case of Jesus, meant crucifixion.

How could such a tragedy happen? How could people be so blind, so stupid? Stephen put his finger

117

on the trouble—they resisted the Holy Spirit. They had their minds set and they would not listen to God.

How do you resist the Holy Spirit? You do it by closing your mind to the Word of God. Whenever we trust in our own wisdom rather than God's, whenever we let our prejudices guide us, we are resisting the Spirit.

Think of those who scorn the poor in our society, despite the fact that the Bible tells us that God loves the poor and seeks to help them. Anyone who looks down on the poor is resisting the Spirit.

We resist the Spirit when we harbor hatred against other people. The Spirit of God tells us that we are to love even our enemies.

We resist the Spirit when we are prejudiced against people of another race, for the Word says there is neither Jew nor Greek but all are one in Christ Jesus.

We resist the Spirit—what a stupid thing to do. God is always right and we must listen and follow his word. The story of what happened to the rulers of Israel is a warning for all of us.

*Holy Spirit, guide me in my day by day living. May I always be willing to listen to your word. In Jesus' name. Amen.*

**Acts 8:14-24**

# NO SALE

The story is an apocryphal one, we hope. The wealthy man who had lived his life separated from God, was on his deathbed. "Reverend," he said to the minister who was visiting him, "I haven't led a

118

very good life. Now I'm dying and I'm afraid to die. Do you think it would help if I gave the church a half a million dollars?"

The minister licked his lips in anticipation. "It's worth a try," he replied softly. The story must be false, for few people would be so foolish as to try such a gimmick even if the temptation would be very strong for a minister to agree to the proposition. Everyone knows that God isn't for sale. He has no need of our money. One wonders at the stupidity of Simon, who thought he could buy the power of the Holy Spirit. Simon was the real "Simple Simon." His name is still used to describe the practice of selling offices in the church—simony.

Yet the temptation to try to bribe God is a strong one. Human beings still try to bargain with God. We say, "If you'll heal me, God, I'll go to church every Sunday." We promise to give up all our bad habits in exchange for a favor from God. We are bargainers at heart. But God is not in the buying and selling business. The Holy Spirit isn't for sale. The cash register rings up "No Sale."

In a beautiful Christmas poem, Christina Rossetti once summed up our relationship with God:

> What can I give Him
> Poor as I am?
> If I were a shepherd,
> I would give a lamb,
> If I were a Wise Man,
> I would do my part, —
> But what can I give Him,
> Give my heart.

That's all God wants from us—our heart, our love. That's all he wanted from Simon. Simon might have had the gift of the Holy Spirit and the power that he wanted. But he tried to buy it and God's gifts aren't for sale.

*Lord, give me the guidance of the Holy Spirit. I have nothing to offer except my love. Amen.*

Acts 8:26-39

# THE QUIET SPIRIT

"You will shout when it hits you, yes indeed." Those words from an old song describe what happened to many of the first Christians when they were converted. When people received the Holy Spirit and were baptized they often talked in tongues or showed other signs that something had happened to them. That occurred in Samaria when Peter and John came to the believers there. It happened to the household of Cornelius and was so plain that the church became convinced that Gentiles also could become believers.

Most churches seem very quiet today. There are no outward signs that anyone has been blessed by the Spirit. After a baptism of a child or an adult the worship service continues at its usual pace. What's the difficulty? Has the Spirit deserted Christians today?

The story of the Ethiopian eunuch provides an answer. We aren't told that he spoke in tongues or experienced some extraordinary happening. He simply went on his way, rejoicing. The Spirit was quiet in his case. Nor is he the only example of the quiet Spirit. There is no mention of any special outbursts when people were baptized at Pentecost. Paul was healed of his temporary blindness but that was all that occurred at his baptism. The jailer at Philippi rejoiced at his baptism but no other signs were shown.

In other words, the Spirit operates in his own way. At times there may be a rather noisy display of power. At times he is quiet, simply bringing joy and peace into the human heart. We must not forget that the Spirit is symbolized by a raging fire and by a fluttering dove. And both are valid signs that the Spirit is present.

There are people today who insist that they have received manifestations of the Spirit, just as people in New Testament times. It is not our business to tell them they are wrong. But no one dare say that the Spirit must operate in a certain fashion. He is free and independent and sometimes he shows his greatest power by quietly stirring the human heart.

*O Holy Spirit, fill me with love toward others and with gratitude toward God. That is all I ask. In Jesus' name. Amen.*

**Acts 13:1-4**

# COMMISSIONED FOR WORK

Every Christian is a minister! Does that seem strange? We are accustomed to think of ministers as people who have attended a seminary and have been ordained for full-time church service. But all believers are to minister to others, to serve others, to help others. You don't have to be ordained before you can tell someone else about your faith or help a needy person or visit someone who is lonely or ill. We are all ministers.

But there are people who have special talents and can serve in special places. And the Holy Spirit calls individuals for such tasks. Paul and Barnabas received a call and were commissioned to do mission work among the heathen and among Jews who had not heard about Jesus Christ. The Spirit called, and then the church commissioned the two men for work. That service in Antioch must have meant a great deal to the two workers. Probably there were times when they wondered, "What am I doing here in this mess?" when life was hard. But then they could remember that the Spirit had called them and the church had commissioned them for special work.

What happened then still happens today. God still uses certain people for unusual work. The church still sends out missionaries to foreign places. It still calls Christians to work full time in congregations and in other areas of Christian service. And the pattern is the same as it was in Paul's day. There must be some conviction on the part of the individual and the church that it is the desire of the Holy Spirit that this person serve in a special capacity. Then the church commissions the individual by the laying on of hands, just as in the beginning.

And there is still great comfort in this ceremony. Being a full-time church worker is no easy task even if the call is not to a foreign land or a difficult parish. So there is strength in remembering that the Spirit and the church had a part in what has occurred. Ministry is for everyone but special ministry requires special help and strength.

*Lord, be with all who work in your church, especially with those who have devoted their lives to your work. Amen.*

# ARROGANCE OR OBEDIENCE

During World War I the Emperor of Germany was often described as arrogant, and one of the accusations laid against him was that he talked about *Ich und Gott,* I and God, as if he had God in his vest pocket. Perhaps the charge was a part of wartime propaganda, but the attitude, I and God, is not an unknown one even for people who aren't rulers or emperors. Religious people often speak as if they have a hotline to heaven and even the church can grow too proud when it poses as God's spokesman. It can be very impressive to say, "Thus saith the Lord," but at times such a declaration arises from the notion that we've got God in a box and he says what we want him to say.

But there is another way to say the same thing. At the first church council, when men were discussing whether or not Gentiles had to become Jews before they could become Christians, the final decision was given in these words: "Is has pleased the Holy Spirit and us." That has a different ring to it. The church leaders allowed themselves to be guided by the Spirit and thus they were saying in all humility and obedience that the Spirit had led and they had concurred.

That's the way it should be—it has pleased the Holy Spirit and us. Sometimes it takes some wrestling before we can come to such a conclusion. Our own ideas are often not in harmony with the Word of God. We have to listen and to yield our will to God. Some in that first church council found the decision a hard one to agree to. They had been trained to believe that salvation was only for the Jews. Perhaps

123

there were some forced smiles when they said, "It has pleased the Holy Spirit and us."

But they did the right thing. They pushed aside their own prejudices and desires and submitted to the leadership of the Spirit. And we must be willing to obey in the same way. It's not I and God. It's the Holy Spirit and us.

*Lord, take away all pride and arrogance from my heart. Help me to follow where the Spirit leads. Amen.*

Acts 19:1-7

# THEY HADN'T HEARD

"We have never even heard that there is a Holy Spirit." What a pity. The people whom Paul met in Ephesus didn't know Jesus Christ had come and they hadn't heard of the Holy Spirit. It wasn't their fault, but they were hopelessly behind the times. How fortunate that Paul could tell them the good news.

But there are still religious people today who live in the same way. They are not aware that the Holy Spirit has come with the news that sins are forgiven, that we are saved by grace alone, that we can have a new life in the Spirit. Instead, these people are busy trying to be saved by keeping the law of God. They gather together their little quota of good deeds, like penguins pulling the stones of Antarctica around their feet. See, I've been to church regularly. Look, I've stopped smoking or swearing.

Even those who have learned to rely on God's

grace often still live as though they had never heard of the Holy Spirit. The Spirit brings life, joy, peace, yet many Christians seem to find no real contentment in their faith. The Spirit-filled Word of God contains many precious promises but they are of no value if you don't know them. Other believers can be a source of joy for us but if we never discuss our faith with them, we miss their help. The Spirit aids us in prayer, but only *if* we pray. The gifts of the Holy Spirit are of no help to us unless we ask for them.

It is said that one of the largest diamonds ever discovered was found in an African hut where children were using it as a playtoy. It was of no value until its worth was recognized. In a similar way it means nothing to say that the Holy Spirit has come unless he has come *to us* and plays a part in our life. The people in Ephesus didn't know any better but we do. Let's not miss the joy of a life that is guided by the Spirit.

*Lord, I thank you for the gift of the Spirit. May I seek his guidance in all that I say and do. Amen.*

Romans 8:26-27

# OUR PRAYER PARTNER

"I was struck speechless." "Words failed me." "I couldn't think of a thing to say." We all have that kind of feeling at times. Fear, love or surprise may be too much for us and cause us to stutter or to remain silent.

Talking to God in prayer may cause such an emotional block. Prayer is very natural but it is also filled

125

with anxieties. God seems so remote, so far above us. We are never quite sure what he wants for us or whether we are asking for the wrong things. And, of course, there are our sins. What right have we, weak and sinful, to ask the God of the universe for help? Even the great prophet Isaiah, when he was caught up into the presence of God, could only cry: "Woe is me! For I am lost; for I am a man of unclean lips."

So we need help when we pray. We need a prayer partner. And Paul assures us that we have such a helper, for he tells us that the Spirit intercedes for us with sighs too deep for words. We are not alone when we pray. The Spirit prays with us.

What a wonderful promise. It means that we don't have to polish our words so that they say exactly what we want. After all, what are words between God and man! God isn't moved by fancy language or correct grammar. Moreover, we don't have to worry for fear that we may pray for the wrong thing. The Spirit will make plain our real desires. God is not concerned whether we are sitting or standing or kneeling when we pray. The Spirit doesn't do any of those things and yet he is heard.

A small boy once tried to tell God what his needs were and finally ended up saying, "You know what I mean." And God does, for the Holy Spirit and God the Father talk the same language. They are the same God and they know what we mean.

Often Christians choose a friend to be a prayer partner so they can pray together for the same goal. That's a good idea, but whether we do that or not, we have a prayer partner—the Holy Spirit.

*Spirit of God, help me when I pray. Guide me to*

*ask for good things and to trust in God's greater wisdom at all times. In Jesus' name. Amen.*

# HOW TO CHOOSE
# A PREACHER

Dwight L. Moody was one of the great lay preachers of the church. He touched the lives of thousands of people through his evangelistic work. Someone once said, with perhaps a touch of exaggeration, that Moody robbed hell of a million souls.

Yet he did not seem to have the necessary talents to make him a great preacher. He was short and dumpy in appearance. His voice was high-pitched, almost squeaky. He only finished the fourth grade in school and his language was consequently very unpolished. He once told a critic: "I'm doing the best I can with the grammar I have. Can you say the same thing?" He was said to be one of the few men in American who could pronounce *Jerusalem* in two syllables. Yet this seemingly untalented man drew crowds of people to hear him in Great Britain and America. Why?

The answer may be the same as that which Paul gave to the Corinthians. Paul confessed that he spoke with weakness, fear, and trembling. His message wasn't presented in plausible words of wisdom. But God's Holy Spirit was with Paul and it was the Spirit that the congregation heard and the Spirit that saved the hearers. Paul and Moody both gave the glory to God.

Not many of us are called to be ministers but all

127

can profit by Paul's words about preaching. It is easy to be impressed by a speaker's voice or appearance or polished language. Some of the preachers on radio and TV have great personal charm. And congregations often choose their ministers solely on the basis of such externals. Of course, God can use preachers with good voices, striking appearance, good education. But first of all there must be a willingness to let the Holy Spirit guide and shine through the message. For it is the Word of God that we want to hear every Sunday and nothing should get in the way of that message.

*Lord, be with the ministers of your church. Enlighten their hearts and minds and give them the power of the Spirit as they speak and live your word. Amen.*

**1 Corinthians 3:16-17**

## THIS HOLY HOUSE

It must have been a magnificent building, that great temple built by Solomon in Jerusalem. It shone with gold and silver and finely carved wood. When the building was finished "the glory of the Lord filled the house of the Lord." The temple was the center of worship in the Old Testament.

When we make comparisons today we usually think of some magnificent cathedral, some gem of architecture built by medieval artisans. And we call such a building "the house of the Lord." And that is all wrong. The New Testament is not interested in buildings. God no longer lives in houses, if he ever did. He lives in you and me. We are the temple of the Lord. The Holy Spirit dwells in us, as Paul reminds us.

That's a wondrous thought. That gray-haired old lady who walks with wavering steps is nevertheless as beautiful as Solomon's temple. That pimply-faced teenager who is finding it difficult to grow up, is nevertheless the temple of the Lord. The slightly overweight and balding man who takes up the collection on Sunday is the temple of the Lord. All people have been created by God, and therefore are temples, places where God's Spirit chooses to dwell.

But that is also a sobering thought. How easily we accept the wonderful thing that is our body. Even if it were only a finely built machine, it would be a shame to misuse it as so many do. But think! God dwells here. God's Spirit is within you.

That should be a guide for us. We must take good care of God's temple. We must not defile it with cheap and tawdry thoughts. We dare not take the temple places where we know the Spirit would not want to go. We must not neglect or misuse our body. It is God's temple.

Walt Whitman once wrote: "I sing the body electric." The Christian should sing the body made holy. Solomon's temple fell into ruins long ago, but the temple of the Holy Spirit remains while we live and we shall live forever.

*Lord, I thank you for the gift of my body. May it always be a place where your Holy Spirit may delight to dwell. Help me to keep body and soul clean and true. Amen.*

129

# CAN YOU SAY THE WORDS?

"Jesus is Lord. Jesus is Lord. Jesus is Lord." There. I've said it three times. What's so hard about that? Why does Paul insist that we need the help of the Holy Spirit to say such a simple expression?

Of course, it's not mere words that Paul is talking about. An atheist could mouth the expression. Paul is speaking about our acknowledging the rulership of Jesus Christ in our life, of our being willing to say, "Have thine own way, Lord, have thine own way." And that's not an easy thing to do.

The difficulty arises because of our human pride. Somehow we want to be Lord, we want to rule. We are willing to give God some place in our life; we are willing to try to love Jesus. But when he insists on being first, when he demands to be Lord of all or Lord not at all, as John Mott once said, we don't like that.

Thus we come to an impasse. We want to be religious but only on a part-time basis. And God doesn't accept such terms. Emil Brunner once put the situation clearly in a sermon:

> There are rooms in order to enter which you must stoop if you are not to knock your head. The cross of Jesus Christ is the door to communion with God and everlasting life. You must stoop if you wish to go in; otherwise you will knock your head and find no admittance.

So we need help. Someone must batter down our pride, someone must show us that there is no other way to be saved except to say, "Jesus is Lord." Enter now the Holy Spirit. Through the Word of God the Spirit shows us our sins. He shows us God's love. He calls us to receive the good things of God by bowing our head and saying, "Jesus is Lord." As Luther puts it: "But the Holy Spirit has called me through the Gospel, enlightened me with his gifts, and sanctified and kept me in the true faith."

Only when we have yielded all to the guidance of the Spirit can we truly say and mean: "Jesus is Lord." Becoming a Christian is the easiest and the most difficult thing in the world. But with the help of the Spirit, everyone can take that step.

*Spirit of God, help me to place my life completely in God's hands. May Jesus always be my Lord. In his name. Amen.*

1 Corinthians 12:4-11

## WHAT CAN YOU DO?

A famous preacher was once told by another minister: "When I listen to you, I tell myself, I'll never preach again."

The famous orator was not taken in by this kind of praise: "That's silly," he declared. "I'm me. You're you. Do the best you can with the gifts God gave you. That's all he expects of anyone."

The speaker was right, of course. God doesn't make us all the same, and no individual excels in everything. Some people can sing beautifully, some can teach others. Some can only sit and listen. But all are important in the work of the church. Paul in his ministry had to deal with all kinds of people and he gave us two important guidelines about talents.

First, all talents come from the Holy Spirit. He makes it possible for us to speak or sing or be good listeners. Since talents are given, no one has any cause to be puffed up or to brag about his or her accomplishments.

This doesn't mean of course that people don't train or work at talents. A gift from God must be cultivated. That's why we have seminaries and voice coaches and schools for those who want to be better preachers, teachers, organists, or church elders. But unless the Spirit has given the gift in the first place, all the training in the world won't help. A crow could spend hours and money training his voice but he would still sound like a crow when he was finished with the training.

Also all talents or gifts are given for the common good of the church. Gifts must be used or they are of no value. Just as a pearl loses its lustre if it is not worn, so God's talents are valuable only when we use them. Paul himself recognized that he owed a debt to both Jews and Gentiles. God had given him the ability to speak and he needed to use it for the good of all.

It is wonderful to be talented. It is a great blessing. But it is also a responsibility for we must acknowledge the source of our ability and the proper use of it for others.

*Lord, I thank you for whatever gifts you have given me. May I never grow proud or neglectful of your blessings. Amen.*

# BOUND BY BAPTISM

When the Vatican Council met a few years ago and began to consider the relationship between Roman Catholics and other Christians, one truth guided their deliberations. All who called themselves Christians had been baptized. Forms and methods might differ but whether people were called Roman Catholics, Lutherans, Methodists or whatever, all had received the water of baptism. That fact caused the delegates to make some gestures of friendship toward other denominations, gestures which people had thought impossible before this great meeting.

Strange that it had taken Christians so long to come to this simple conclusion. For all who bear Christ's name have received the same sacrament and baptism itself has only one source—the Holy Spirit. Thus all Christians are bound together by a common custom and by a common source of power. Perhaps we have quarreled too much about the method and the time when baptism is administered and have thus lost sight of its binding nature.

Baptism acquaints us with the real democracy in the church. People are baptized because they are sinners, because they all need the cleansing of this water. No matter who we are, Jews or Greeks, slaves or free, as Paul says, we need this sacrament. Every baptized person says to the world: "I'm a sinner." It is the badge of our unity.

And baptism also speaks of the source of power. It is the Holy Spirit who does the work. Jesus told Nicodemus that a man must be born again of "water and Spirit" almost as if the two were one. Baptism

133

is not something we do but something we receive. As Luther reminds us:

> It is not water that does these things, but God's Word with the water and our trust in this Word. Water by itself is only water, but with the Word of God it is a life-giving water which by grace gives the new birth through the Holy Spirit.

Bound by baptism. We say that something is as weak as water, but when the Spirit of God is involved the water of baptism holds together the church of God.

*Lord, I thank you for my baptism. May it remind me of my fellowship with all Christians. Amen.*

**Galatians 5:16-25**

## TWO WAYS OF BLOWING

A young boy started to work for a new employer. He noticed his master blowing on his hands. "What are you doing that for?" he asked.

"I'm blowing on my hands to warm them up," was the reply.

Later that day, at the dinner table the boy saw his boss blowing on some soup. "Why are you doing that?" he asked.

"To cool off my soup. It's too hot."

"I quit," said the boy. "I refuse to work for a man who can blow both hot and cold." That's a silly story and yet what it says is true. Human beings can blow both hot and cold. People can write beautiful poetry, sing tuneful songs and paint exciting pictures. They can also steal and lie and rape and kill. And the same person can do both things, can blow hot and cold.

Paul describes this double nature by listing the works of the flesh and the works of the Spirit. The contrast is startling, immorality, impurity, licentiousness, etc. vs. love, joy, peace, patience, etc.

What makes the difference? Are some people born corrupt and others good? No. The potential for good or evil exists in everyone. Is it a matter of deciding to do good or to do evil? Not that either. It is the Spirit of God who makes the difference. If we allow the Spirit to come into our life, then good things follow. If on the other hand we simply let nature take its course, if we let our human desires rule, then the dark side of human nature will show itself.

The contrast is sharp and clear. There is no middle ground, for either you are led by the Spirit or you aren't. For while the same person may be able to blow both hot and cold physically, no one can be led by the flesh and the Spirit at the same time. It is an awesome choice that we must make, for or against the Spirit. But as Paul knew so well, God will give us the power to choose the right.

*Holy Spirit, help me this day and every day to be guided by you. May I seek and bear the good fruits of life. In Jesus' name. Amen.*

Ephesians 1:13-14

## THE ENGAGEMENT RING

Times have changed but it is still accepted custom for a young man to give an engagement ring to his fiance. And girls still delight in showing off this symbol of love. But unless the bride-to-be is totally greedy, the engagement ring is valued, not for what it cost but for what it means. An engagement ring speaks of the future. It stands for a new home, a life with someone who is loved, perhaps even a family in the years ahead.

Strangely enough, the Holy Spirit resembles an engagement ring. You can't hock him in a pawn shop, but he is valuable to us, not just for what it means now but for what he promises for the future.

Christians are sometimes disturbed at the contrast between what Jesus promised and what his followers receive. Jesus spoke of glory and promised that those who love him should partake of that glory. We know that Jesus himself is now seated at the right hand of God the Father and is partaking of heavenly glory. But all too often the Christian must face trouble and tribulation. We may feel like the famous saint who told God: "If this is the way you treat your friends, no wonder you have so few of them." Even if our life here is relatively undisturbed, it seems to fall far short of the promised glory and bliss.

But we have the Holy Spirit. He is the pledge that Jesus will keep his word. He is the assurance that God's good things will eventually be ours. Like an engagement ring, the Holy Spirit promises that there is more ahead for us, glory, blessing and joy.

And so, just as a woman may gaze at her engagement ring and dream of the joy that marriage will bring, so we can see in the Holy Spirit the promise, the earnest money of the future. As Paul wrote to the Corinthians: "Eye hath not seen nor ear heard, neither have entered into the heart of man, the things which God hath prepared for them that love him" (KJV). But we have the Spirit.

*Thank you, Lord, for sending me the Holy Spirit. When I grow discouraged, he comforts me. When I grow weary he promises me rest and joy. Thank you. Amen.*

Ephesians 4:1-6

# THERE'S ONLY ONE!

Omar Khayyam wrote about "the Two-and-Seventy jarring sects" of his day. But Christianity has long since eclipsed that number. No one can be sure how many separate church organizations exist today but Christians have long since passed the two hundred mark and the number keeps growing.

Some of the divisions in Christianity are the result of history and geography but many churches have come into existence because of the sinful actions of human beings. Stubbornness, pride, and the desire to be different have plagued the church almost from the beginning. And despite recent efforts to promote church unity, the healing of the divisions proceeds so slowly.

Most of us can't do much about this. Christian unity is a very difficult and complicated subject. But there is something we can do. We can stress the source of unity—the Holy Spirit. It is the Spirit that is supposed to guide the churches, and there is only one Spirit. There isn't a Holy Spirit for the Baptists and another one for Lutherans. That means that others outside our own group may also speak God's truth.

It is important then that we listen to what the Spirit says through and to other Christians. Too often we look on other Christians as inferior to us, not quite up to our high standards. As one minister was supposed to have said when reminded by another that we serve the same God: "Yes, you in your way and I in his." That's not the way to achieve Christian fellowship. We must learn to hear the Spirit speaking in the language of others.

One Spirit. That's all there is. And as Paul reminds us, that Spirit gives us one hope. All Christians hope some day to be united with Jesus Christ and to live with him through all eternity. Isn't it time that we prepare for that day by being guided by the same Spirit here on earth?

> How good it is for brethren
> Who know each other well,
> In unity together
> On this fair earth to dwell!

*Lord, may I put aside all pride and prejudice and join in praising you with all who hear and heed your Spirit. Amen.*

**1 Timothy 4:1-5**

# NEVERTHELESS, A GOOD CROP

Every year church statistics report the gains and losses in local congregations and in larger church groups. And when such reports are published there is always a sharp reaction. If more members are lost than gained, a great outcry goes up that the church

138

is collapsing. Even if there has been some growth church officials usually do some breast-beating because a number of members have been placed on the inactive list.

Of course it is sad when people fall away. Yet the Bible warns us that this will happen. In the Parable of the Sower, Jesus described how some seed would spring to life and then wither away in the hot sun, and some plants would be choked out by the weeds of this world. Paul told Timothy the same thing. He said the Spirit was prophesying that the people would turn away from the truth and listen to false teachers.

Perhaps we need to listen to the Spirit in this matter too. It should never bring us joy when someone drops out of church, even if that person is a troublemaker, for all need the gospel. Yet it is possible to get terribly discouraged because of losses in the church. You can feel like Elijah who thought everyone had turned to Baal except him. Even the minister on Sunday morning can stand before the congregation and see the people who aren't there rather than the faithful ones who have gathered for worship.

The warning given by the Spirit is important. He says some will fall away. Some will join strange sects and embrace peculiar teachings. That makes us sad. But the Holy Spirit also gives us another picture in the Book of Revelation:

> After this I looked, and behold, a great multitude which no man could number, from every nation, from all tribes and peoples and tongues, standing before the throne and before the Lamb, clothed in white robes, with palm branches in their hands, crying out with a loud

voice, "Salvation belongs to our God who sits upon the throne, and to the Lamb" (Rev. 7:9-10).

The harvest which the Spirit promises us will be a rich one. Let's never forget that picture.

*Lord, keep your church from false teachings and your people from deceitful leaders. May we never forget that the victory is yours. Amen.*

**2 Peter 1:19-21**

# NO ORDINARY BOOK

The Bible looks like an ordinary book, particularly when it is printed in the same style as other publications. The Bible reads like an ordinary book, for it uses words and sentences in the same fashion as a novel or the daily newspaper. Yet Christians have always regarded the Bible as a unique message from God, and the author of the Second Epistle of Peter tells us that the writers of the Scriptures spoke under the direction of the Holy Spirit. How are we to understand this?

Perhaps we can grasp the answer by observing the parallel with the one whom we call the *Word*, Jesus Christ. When Jesus was here on earth, people saw him as a man, a human being, nothing more. They were impressed by his striking way of speaking and his ability to heal, but no one on casual acquaintance thought of him as divine. Even the disciples didn't realize Jesus' true nature for much of his ministry.

Yet those who knew Jesus best gradually began to

realize there was something different about him. When they listened they heard God talking to them. Jesus was human, but he was more than that. He was also the Son of God.

The Bible has the same dual nature. The casual reader may consider it just another book, at times inspiring and at times terribly dull. Critics may poke fun at the Word and scoff at the idea that God had a hand in it. But those who read the Bible carefully and prayerfully become aware that this is no ordinary book. The Spirit of God speaks to us through these pages. The ancient words of the Bible present us with a message from God.

When a monarch is crowned in England, the Archbishop of Canterbury gives the ruler a copy of the Bible and says, "We present you with this book, the most valuable thing that this world affords. Here is wisdom; here is the royal law; here are the lively oracles of God." The Archbishop can say those words because the Spirit of God had a part in writing this book.

*Lord, teach me to love your Word. May I hear in this ancient book the clear voice of the Holy Spirit speaking to me. Amen.*